UNDERSTANDING

CHANGE

And

Being a Competent Resource for Your
Dependents in a Changing Society

Albert R. de Goias M. D.

ITMAC Corporation - Toronto

Canadian Cataloguing in Publication Data
De Goias, Albert R
    Understanding Change.
Bibliography: p. Includes Index.
1. Stress Management.
2. Personnel Management.
3. Family Management.
ISBN 0-9694351-0-X

Editorial contribution: M. O. De Goias
Typesetting: Siegfried Betterman.
Printed and bound in Canada by T.H. Best Printing Company Limited.

Acknowledgements.

The author gratefully acknowledges the contributions of people who, regrettably, can only be mentioned in this first section, but who played a greater role in the formation of the whole manuscript than can be documented.

Margaret de Goias was instrumental in the research of all sociological data and for editing the flow of ideas from the first draft through as many as ten subsequent drafts before the final manuscript was made ready for publication. I gratefully acknowledge her contribution.

Terrence Russell, first as human resources manager at the Royal Bank of Canada, and later as my close friend and confidant, helped me formulate my ideas from their inception as a stress management tool to their final stage as a tool for people to manage other people.

Dr. Jan Kryspin, professor of family medicine at the University of Toronto, saw the value in my first attempts to address the issue, encouraged me to start organizing my work for publication, and arranged for the first and second publication of research material.

Dr. Ian McWhinney, professor of family medicine at the University of Western Ontario, was an essential force in assessing the ideas from the perspective of the clinician, and showing me how to go about researching and publishing them.

Alison Pearce, past school principal and presently a school trustee, who arranged for me to be exposed to the educational media through which some of my later research material was obtained.

I wish to thank my wife, Margaret, who helped in perhaps the most difficult part of this labor of eight years, supporting me when nothing seemed to be going right, and understanding when I was so tired that I snapped at everything in sight. My son, Darren unwittingly contributed, first by being such a challenge in his early years, and then by becoming the self directed youth he has turned out to be in his later years. My daughter, Rochelle contributed unselfishly by always being willing to share her consideration and concern whenever she saw the tiredness and disappointments that were so closely associated with the development of this work.

To all of these people, and to all of those who couldn't be mentioned, I give my heartfelt thanks.

Preface

This book is designed, not as a strategy for managing change, but as a way of managing the more flexible component in dealing with change, the human potential. It is not as much a strategy for managing people as it is an educational tool for knowing how people naturally respond to unwanted change, and how to steer them into recognizing and using their potential in an environment which changes more rapidly than they have learned to accept.

The manager is defined as the person who is willing to take responsibility for seeing a task to its conclusion. It is the intent of this book to show that this can be a rewarding and exciting adventure, not just a burden that one must bear.

Of course, if you are a manager of people, it is important to be able to teach this attitude to them so that they too can be independent operators, and either help you extend your reach, or relieve you of responsibilities they can manage themselves.

This is why this book approaches the subject by educating the reader in the general details many of us take for granted. To the reader who does not know these details, they are made available. To the reader who knows them even in greater depth than they are discussed here, these details are offered in a way that he (she) can see share them with the people he (she) manages.

UNDERSTANDING CHANGE

Table of Contents

List of Plates

Introduction.

This text is prepared, not as a training manual, but as a resource manual for those people who must manage competently without assistance, who are in positions of authority over other people, or who are required to lead or direct other people in conditions of change or uncertainty.

It is not absolutely essential to the full understanding of this text to read it in the sequence as it is laid out. Preferably, the text will be used as a reference text. Because of the difficult and pervasive nature of the subject, however, we find it necessary to introduce explanations of how certain things that are blindly accepted as stable, changes. These will provide less informative reading than the rest of the text, and can be read simple for completeness of information.

Many people will find that the last chapters pertaining to their needs, either chapter 8,or chapter 10, will be read first. This will not detract from the intent of the book. They will find, however, that they will need to acquire information from the preceding chapters in order to make full use of these two. Then, they can read the last chapters again, allowing them to make more sense.

It is hoped that this book will be kept as a reference text for use as a counselling tool in addition to its use as a personal educational tool. On the next page, you will find a roadmap to the use of this book. You may use it, or you may choose to read the book in a proper sequence. Whatever you choose, it is hoped that the information contained herein will show you how to hone your own management skills and be a competent resource for the people who can use your skill and expertise.

A GUIDE TO GETTING INFORMATION FROM THIS BOOK MOST EFFECTIVELY.

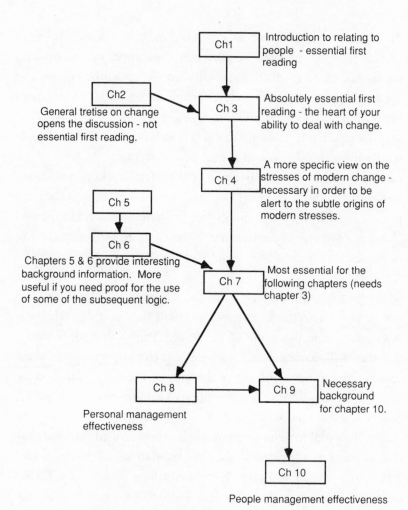

Ch1 — Introduction to relating to people - essential first reading

Ch2 — General tretise on change opens the discussion - not essential first reading.

Ch 3 — Absolutely essential first reading - the heart of your ability to deal with change.

Ch 4 — A more specific view on the stresses of modern change - necessary in order to be alert to the subtle origins of modern stresses.

Ch 5

Ch 6 — Chapters 5 & 6 provide interesting background information. More useful if you need proof for the use of some of the subsequent logic.

Ch 7 — Most essential for the following chapters (needs chapter 3)

Ch 8 — Personal management effectiveness

Ch 9 — Necessary background for chapter 10.

Ch 10 — People management effectiveness

Chapter 1.

The Manager.

Perhaps, the most demanding task you can be asked to do in to-day's society is that of relating to other people from a mature and knowledgeable perspective, or guiding, training, or managing them with authority and consideration. This is because each person is an individual who is influenced by the things which affect him or her personally. It also is because you live in a vast and complex environment, so vast that the other people can be affected by parts of the environment that may be totally alien to your experience, and so complex that even those parts that are familiar to you will have areas that you cannot see. It is this combination of the individuality of people and the complexities of the challenge that makes manag-ing or even relating to other people a difficult and frequently unre-warding experience.

Yet, you do it. You may be managing people in a business organization, guiding children in a family, or training students in a school. You may be responsible for the well being of people in a community or clients in an office. You simply may be the person who takes the more responsible position in relating to another person such as a spouse, a friend, or a colleague.

You do this, not because you have more advanced skills or more than adequate preparation than these other people. Sometimes, you arrive at this position because you are a little more experienced at a particular task or more familiar with a particular event than the people around you. Sometimes you are just a little less confused, tired, or deflated than that other person or those other people.

In any case, you must be able to recognize that the most frequent cause of disharmony, hostility, or stress in any relationship between two or more people is the inability of one of the people involved in a confrontation to take the mature position and approach the unknown and unfamiliar aspect of the situation without feeling threatened, or consider the other's perspectives without resentment. If you see stress as a condition which exists when what you have to do exceeds what you have for doing it, you will recognize that relating to people or managing them can easily be regarded as the most frequent way of reaching this imbalance.

In other words, one person must be willing to take charge and guide the other person in order to manage the confrontation or the common responsibility. Even if you are not in a traditional position of management, by taking the mature position in a relationship, you will have accepted the responsibility of 'managing' the other person.

This can be an unfair burden on you. The complexities of the common environment affect you just as harshly as they do the other person. The desire to be respected without compromise is as important to you as it is to the other people.

Yet, if you wish to succeed in the task you have chosen to do, or which you have inherited by virtue of your position, you must be able to have, as your main objective, the development of that other person or those other people into more capable and more productive members of society or of the unit in which you function.

You must be able to manage your own challenges capably even

though these challenges are no less complex than those the other people have to manage. You must be able to be a resource for the people who look to you for guidance, assistance, or consideration, even though the problems they have to manage are rarely greater than or coincident with yours.

This may seem to be a difficult or impossible task. You must remember, however, that you live in a world of people. The whole direction of everything you do, everything you plan, is influenced by how it allows you to relate to other people.

Thus, unless you can relate to these people from a position of greater insight and understanding, their fears and the defenses they use to counteract these fears will become excessive burdens for you to bear.

Unless you can nurture them into being fully responsible for what they do and how well they succeed, they will always be there to demand more of you, drain you, or leave you with the responsibility for their unfinished tasks.

The extra work which may be required initially in order either to motivate or educate these people may be seen as an investment towards your greater peace of mind. If they can acquire a greater awareness of the problem and if they are motivated to accept responsibility for managing it, they can propel themselves into being more competent than you may have anticipated, and so manage the task more efficiently, or approach the confrontation with less hostility.

Then, the communications you will have established with them will suppress future problems before they arise as these people will more likely approach you with early difficulties or discuss weaknesses with you rather than compound their problems with the effects of their frustrations.

In short, the role of the more responsible person or the person in the more responsible position is to be the leader, and to know how to lead when conditions are strange or in turmoil as well as when they are familiar or stable. Whether you want it or not, there are times when you must assume the role of the more responsible person. It is up to you to do it efficiently and effectively. Even if you are simply taking the mature role in your relation to another adult from an intimate stance, you have accepted the role of manager, albeit for a temporary period.

Management - the objective of the responsible person.

If you are going to manage a task, you will take control of that task and guide it with skill and authority towards a specific objective. If that task is a problem that is easily identifiable, and the objective is one which is easily reachable, you will be able to manage it effectively without too much bother or difficulty.

If the task is even a little more complex or the objective a little less reachable so that a tool or machine is required to take the task to the objective, you still can manage it as long as you have developed the skill and expertise in using that tool or machine.

When, however, the task is the productivity and capability of another human being, and the objective is such a complex factor as the efficient management of some part of this vast and constantly changing common environment, success becomes a little more elusive. When the tool or machine for reaching that task (the person's capabilities) is also the independently activated skills, training, and ambition of the person himself (herself), management becomes governed by a totally different set of rules. It no longer can be the simple application of one rule that has worked somewhere else. Nor is it the attempts to seduce the person with prizes that may have attracted someone else. Rather, it is the ability to approach each person as an indivuidual and each task as a complex interplay of multiple factors, to be managed, not by pretending that one or the other can be made to be stable, but by attempting to understand them as they change.

Thus, if you believe that the task of managing other people lies in being able to manipulate them as implements for you to reach the common objective, you also will see that success is made complex and frequently impossible by the very independent nature of the implements. If, however, you see the task of managing or relating to people as guiding these other people into managing their responsibilities themselves, or into producing effective solutions which can be shared and applied to the common responsibility, you will perhaps be more prepared to solve the two most difficult aspects of this management problem, those of identifying the task and using the tools.

Since, at this point, you are interested in how the other person is able to manage the problem, your challenge is not the problem but the person, namely that person's capacity for managing the problem. This is something you cannot measure. You cannot measure where any single person begins. You cannot measure how far that person may have developed. You know only that each person begins at point zero, and that each person progresses at an independent rate. That person's capabilities are hidden, known only to himself (herself).

As a responsible person, you have a task to accomplish, but the task has not been properly defined because you cannot be sure where your starting point is or even whether you will have completed the task.

In addition, even this ill defined task of guiding other people or another person into becoming more capable or productive is further compounded by the independence with which each person may activate his (her) skills and desires. The tools, that is, the skills, knowledge, and motivation of the people themselves, which you must use to help them manage a problem effectively are not accessible to you.

The human being is a self driven force. He (she) cannot be turned on and off, or intentionally guided as can be done with a machine like a motorcar. The human being cannot be loaded with immediately relevant information and used to manipulate that infomation as can be done with a computer. The human being is so independent that, regardless of how urgently you may need his or her performance, you cannot simply make it happen. You must wait for that person to want to produce, and to accept responsibility for the management of the task. It is this combination of the undetermined task added to the inaccessible tools that makes people management the most difficult management task there is.

The objective of Management.

The ultimate objective in the management of any task is usually the attempt to improve its presentation, the way we see it anyway. In a similar way, the ultimate objective in managing another human being is the attempt to improve his or her presentation of his or her skills and understanding. This translates as improved productivity in business, improved social awareness in families, improved consideration in friendship, and improved educational skills in schools.

You will see later that the main asset of the human being is that person's ability to make a contribution to the world by formulating ideas and expressing them. In short, people must be productive.

People are not born productive. We are born, however, with the capacity to be productive. When that capacity is nurtured, the human being becomes more than an extension of a person with greater vision, of a business, or of society in general. He or she becomes a self-driven source of information and perception.

If, then, the ultimate objective of managing or relating to other people is to nurture their understanding of a particular situation and help them to be more productive, the task of management becomes the task of being a competent authority on the areas in which you must lead them, being able to communicate with them, and being able to motivate them to share your vision and manage their tasks competently and independently.

It must be done in that sequence. Remember, you cannot reach the tools. You must reach people and stimulate them into using their tools. You cannot store your information into other people or inject them with your skills. You must let them use the tools which they have and which you have helped them activate to increase their knowledge and skills to accomplish the task.

Of course, this means that you must be able, not only to guide the other people, but to allow them full responsibility for accomplishing the task, you being only the facilitator to the development of their capacity for making that accomplishment. Thus, the objective of people management is the development of other people, not using them as extensions of yourself.

If you can accept that your task, in managing or relating to another person, is the nurturing of that other person, and in order to accomplish that task you need to learn how to reach and facilitate that person's independence, you will have realized the most important difference between the management of a physical task and the management of people.

The abstract nature of people as a task requires that you approach them with respect for their personal visions, recognition of their developed skills and understanding, and faith in their potential as independent human beings.

Of course, this means that on the other side of your desk sits a force that may already be a formidable asset, or one which can be nurtured into being such an asset with the proper respect and guidance.

Usually, therefore, it is a cinch to manage people or to take the mature role in relating to them. Unlike the car or the computer which needs your direct input in order for them to produce anything, people, by being self driven, are theoretically capable of holding their own and managing the task with their own initiative.

Theoretically, at least, the management of people is the ability to delegate effectively and to let those self driven forces complete their apportioned tasks. Practically, however, only a small segment of any group of people are so dependable. The rest, for one reason or another, require that they be activated in order for them to function effectively. They then become a challenge to you.

The Alternative to Management.

It seems that it is not always necessary for you to take the mature position and manage the people for whom you are responsible or to whom you wish to relate. You may, for instance, take the alternative of finding the right person who will fit into the job easily, one who has desires and expectations that are coincident with yours, or one who is able to anticipate your desires and strive to satisfy them.

Then, you can discharge the person who is not pulling his or her weight and replace that person with another more competent person. You may send your defiant or obstreperous child to a distant aunt's or to a military academy for training and discipline. You may divorce your inconsiderate or incompatible spouse and seek a more compatible mate.

This is not the intent of this work, however. For one thing, it is difficult to find sufficient quantities of highly motivated and self driven individuals to replace the poorly productive ones and expect that they will remain motivated as conditions change. For another, you will find that the new person will become just as difficult to manage or to relate to when conditions change further and surpass his (her) developed resources. The only easy person to manage or relate to is the one who can adapt himself (herself) to the demands of the changing conditions. This is difficult to find in just anybody. It, however, is easier to develop in a person, or have that person develop in himself (herself).

The Challenge of Managing or Relating to People Successfully.

For reasons to be discussed later, many people are so easily inundated by the demands of today's environment that too many of them cannot continue to face these changing challenges with self driven accountability and motivation. They need to be managed.

This is not to say that these people are unable to take charge and manage in other areas. The fact is that, in this vast and complex environment, the most capable people will, at some point, be challenged by situations that are outside of their range. When that happens, even they will need help to manage their problems or consideration for their opinions.

Obviously, this also can happen to you. Sometimes, it can happen to both people in a confrontation at the same time. The point, however, is that one person must decide to take the mature position and manage or guide the other. In this argument, that person is you.

This is your task if you are a parent. This is your task if you are the teacher. This also is your task if you are a business manager who wants to have a job done efficiently and effectively. By and large, it also has become your task if you are in a confrontation with your spouse, associate, or colleague, and if you want either to benefit from your association with that other person or avoid having to deal with his or her unnecessary defenses.

Regardless of the area in which you manage or relate to people, you no longer have a choice. If you are responsible for other people's productivity, you must learn to manage them, not just expect adequate performance from them. If you are responsible for the management of a common responsibility in association with another person or other people, you must learn to manage these people, not just expect compatibility with them. You must learn to accept as your task, not the common responsibility, but the persons with whom you must face the common responsibility.

You must know that just as the inefficient and defensive person can become productive and considerate so too can the efficient and considerate person be inefficient and defensive under different circumstances. Thus, the task of managing and relating to people can be a dynamic and challenging one. This may be a stressful responsibility for some people, or an exciting challenge for others.

If you see it as a stressful experience, it may be because you see other people as extensions to yourself with you being their driving force, an exhausting approach to the task of management, or one that loses out on the contributions of the other people. It may be because you see them as being capable, yet being lazy or stupid, and therefore, an unnecessary burden when they require assistance or guidance. If this is the case, you must reassess your perceptions of people.

If you see it as an exciting challenge, you are ready to relate to people positively and manage that association with efficiency and to greater mutual benefit.

You then must be willing to learn how to acknowledge an unmeasurable force even as it continues to grow or regress. You must be willing to help a self-driven force move forward even though it will not progress without help in starting yet will not start if not given the freedom to continue on its own.

The Prerequisite for Successful People Management.

If you were about to use a new machine or to put together a new structure, the first thing you will do is to read the instruction manual. Before you unwittingly do something to destroy a delicate instrument, you will become familiar with the function of its parts. Before you decide to use it to do a particular job, you must ascertain whether it is designed for that job.

It is the same with the management of people. There are two great differences, however. The first is that, unlike a machine which comes off a production line and is designed to be similar to other machines of its type, each human being is a distinct individual.

Every parent knows that each child is different from the other, even if two of them are twins. Every teacher knows that each child is an individual, even if he or she attends the same classes and is given the same homework as the other.

People are so distinct that whatever you may have learned about one person is completely irrelevant for another. In simple terms, relating to another person is similar to having to put together a new machine, each machine being singularly unique and having its own distinct parts and unique operations.

If you intend to put together each machine to have it work efficiently, you are required to read its specific instruction manual. If you try to put them together or use them without reading the instructions, you may damage sensitive parts. In the same way, if you approach the task of managing or relating to people without being prepared to read the instructions that are unique for each person, you will damage very sensitive areas.

People, however, are also private individuals. What they think, what they feel, what they are able to do are facilities that are hidden within them, and which they guard rather possessively. The instruction manual is not easily accessible. It is privately retained within each person. The only way to get at it is to have each person reveal it to you.

As you know, there are good reasons for people's protectionism. When people are challenged by a task, they know that whatever they do is going to be seen as a representation of their true capabilities for managing that task. When people are sure that their capabilities are strong enough to be revealed with pride, they will do so.

When, however, people are challenged to reveal capabilities which may be inadequately developed, or inappropriate for the situation, rather than show their inadequacies or be open to further criticism, they may restrain their opinions and expressions.

These restrained capabilities are possessions which no one can extract from a person without his or her express permission. And no person is willing to give that permission easily to just anybody, especially someone whom they do not know, with whom they may have a disagreement, or who has authority over them.

As the person in the more responsible role, you are expected to manage a task that is different from every other task, one which has no obvious instruction manual.

There is no common pattern which helps you to determine how to approach a particular person or group of people and overcome the need for an instruction manual. There is no instrument which can allow you to read what other people know or what they are thinking. You, therefore, must be able to encourage them to share their instruction manual with you, before you can relate to them without damaging sensitive areas.

This means being competent in the field in which you are leading them, being considerate of their perceptions and opinions, and being willing to assist them in nurturing their independence rather than trying to protect their weaknesses.

The Rules of Successful People Management.

In order to manage that 'task' then, you first must be able to be competent in the issues that affect these other people even as conditions change or become uncertain.

You must recognize that, by relating to a self driven force, your first task is to understand the issues that they are trying to solve. To be such a resource in a changing environment, you must be prepared to expect more of yourself than basic experience. You must be willing to respect change and educate yourself on new problems and new twists in old problems as they continue to invade your familiar tasks. Then educate yourself on how people tend to deal with similar interferences to their familiar issues. This is the first rule of relating to people from a mature perspective - Be a competent resource. Understand your world as it changes, and so be strong in conditions that are fragile or constantly changing. Understand people as they try to deal with a changing world, and be capable in areas that confuse and threaten them.

Secondly, you must know that different people have different perceptions of the common issue. Although their opinions and expressions may be in conflict with those you believe to be right, they also are not wrong. You must be able to communicate with those people, genuinely interested in learning their perceptions of the common issue and the opinions they may have formed from those perceptions. Then, you must be prepared to adapt your opinions to include the new information as it becomes available to you, both from your examination of the issues and from your consideration of the other people's perspective.

Lastly, you must recognize that each person has the capacity to expand his or her visions of the common issue and to manage it independently. All they need is to access their tools of reason, judgement, and past personal experience and apply them appropriately to manage the unknown (to them) situation. You must be able to motivate these other people to manage the issues that affect them. You may need to share greater options with them. You may need to help them overcome their fears and weaknesses. You may need to give them full responsibility for their successes and for the consequences of their failures.

Epilogue.

The main thrust of this book has been directed at placing you, the reader, in the position of final responsibility. You have been given information that allows you to manage independently, above the need for feedback or assistance from other people. This is not to encourage you to be superior to others or isolated from them. Rather, it is to place you in the position of being more useful while also allowing you to have full control over your successes.

You know that you are attracted to people who are both capable and considerate, more than you are attracted to insecure or selfish people. This book gives you that opportunity to be the capable and considerate person to whom the other people around you will be attracted. This shows you how to relate to these others, either at their level, or as an advisor, helping them to become capable and considerate themselves.

It is a known axiom that if you do not need something, you wil not be disappointed by not having it. By learning to be independent in change, you will be strong at times when you will not get anything from the people around you anyway. If you do receive it, let it be icing on the cake. For goodness sake, at least, have a cake first. Then, when you do not receive it, you are, at least, capable of sharing it.

Chapter 2.

The reality of change.

We live in a difficult and demanding world. This is because everything about us is constantly moving. Many people do not always recognize this constant movement until something happens to disrupt their familiar environment. Then they frequently are surprised by the new problems that have evolved, and upset by the demands these changes impose on them.

Yet, the seeds for such disruption are sown constantly, and are growing right before our eyes. Things are happening even to those areas of our environment that seem safe and permanent, changes that almost guarantee their disruption, and we are oblivious to the activities that produce these changes.

Some of these changes happen beyond our awareness. Some of them, we cause, turning a blind eye to the accumulating problems that we can avoid for the moment. The accumulating discards polluting our environment, the progressive liver damage in an alcoholic, the build up of resentment in a neglected relationship all attest to this aspect of change that we can manage if only we would pay attention to those things we cannot understand easily. In the same way, there are things which we do not cause but which we would be able to manage if we would examine them with curiosity rather than attempt to create a world which changes only in the direction we choose.

There are three distinct areas in everyone's life from which change evolves. One of these is nature, or the material environment. Another is the body, or the personal biological environment. The third is people, or the social environment.

The Physical Environment: Vast and Constantly Changing.

As a human being, you relate to your physical environment using five special instruments called senses. If you can see something, hear it, touch it, taste it, or smell it, you know that it is there. It is the only way in which you can be aware of the material world and function within it. Without those senses, you may as well be dead.

When something to which you can relate, or which you can measure with your senses has changed, and that change can be picked up by those instruments, you are aware of the change. When that change cannot be measured by those instruments, you are not aware of the change, even if it has occurred. These senses are sophisticated instruments. Yet, they are far from perfect.

Just think. You may be able to read the words on this page. However, between this page and your eyes, there are billions of small particles. These particles may be microbes, dust particles, or even the molecules of air. We know now that these are real entities even though we did not think so in ancient times.

You know that they are real because if there are enough of them joined together, and they form a large enough mass, you will see the mass. Yet, you cannot see these small particles. You cannot see a fungus, for instance, as a microbe. Yet, if there is a large quantity of these small microbes on a piece of food, you will see the mass. Many people are familiar with the tell tale greenish discoloration on a piece of bread that they know to be fungus.

If change occurs at the level of these submicroscopic entities, you cannot be aware of change, at least not until it has accumulated to the stage at which your senses can be stimulated. Even now, change must be taking place in the chair you are occupying, or in the floor on which that chair rests. It is because of these invisible changes that you eventually will see the process of aging, the fading of color in the material, the accumulation of dust on the floor.

Do you not think that before an earthquake, there is not a buildup of gradual, accumulative changes in the earth's crust? In fact, you know for sure that this is the case. These changes are caused by activities which, in isolation, cannot be recognized by your imperfect instruments. When these activities have caused sufficient change in the objects you can measure, only then can you recognize their presence.

Why it is usual to be unprepared for change in the material environment.

Can you imagine how difficult it will be to live in this world if your eyes were accurate enough to let you see everything that exists in the space before them? You will not be able to recognize anything beyond those that are immediately before your eyes. In that case, an instrument which is too sensitive can be a severe disadvantage. Then, the old adage of not being able to see the forest for the trees will take on a truly realistic meaning.

Can you imagine how disturbing it will be to be able to hear all the sounds that are available to your ears at this very moment? Perhaps, while reading this, you may listen carefully to sounds you have not been hearing because they are occurring at a subliminal level. Then, you may even imagine the discomforts you will experience if your ears can hear more than those sounds, the chirping of every insect, the squeaking of every joint, the rumble of every breeze.   You never will be able to focus on anything important while there is such constant interference from all the activities that are present.

The ability to be aware of all the activities that are occurring in even the most isolated area of this world can be enough to torture any person.   Yet, no isolated area can begin to reveal even the smallest percentage of the vast range of activities that are occurring in all parts of this immense and varied environment.

What happens if you ignore the presence of these activities.

Why, then, you might ask, are these activities allowed to continue unchallenged so that our comfort can be disrupted and our safety threatened? Why can we not use the universal intelligence of mankind and create a dust free, microbe free environment that stays familiar and stable? To some readers these may be seen as superfluous questions.   To many others, however, they are logical and worth consideration. We may not always see the problems the way they are described by these questions. We do, however, go about trying to rid the world of a particular disease, to establish a homogeneous society, or to create materials that will not disintegrate.

You must remember that, in the early ninety sixties, dream designs of the home of the future were suggested with the promise that the next generation will not have to work at keeping the house clean, cooking, or washing utensils. They had visions, then, of unending resources that will provide those opportunities.

Theoretically, when the familiar and comfortable environment was disrupted, we would be able to discard the changed material and replace it with a refreshed version of the original. The throwaway society was born.

People did not see this as hanging on to stability. In fact, many people saw it as being capable of change. If you examine it, you will see, instead, that it was the re-changing of the changed material so that a sameness could be restored. We have learned, however, that these invisible activities accumulate and stay with us.

You are seeing the shattering of the utopian dream: pollution that has arisen from accumulated unseen discards, the greenhouse effect from unseen accumulations of carbon dioxide. These are not new things. They have always been there. We only have allowed them to accumulate because we believed that, by hiding the change, we will not have to deal with it. Now we have so much of it to deal with that it has become an unmanageable stress on us. You can see that we cannot create such a utopian environment, one which is stable, secure, or familiar, because we cannot eliminate those invisible but powerful activities that constantly change it. You also know that we cannot presume that, just because we cannot see these activities, they do not exist.

Change is the reason for an old Egyptian proverb which says, "No man swims the same river twice." Think of it! If you can accept such constant and random fluidity of this environment, you will be able to expect the change that it assuredly will bring to your more familiar tasks and structures. Then, you will learn to allow your surprise to be generated only when that change does not arise.

II The Body: A Biological Marvel in a Delicate and Constantly Changing Balance.

Take your body as another example. Do you know how much activity is going on in it at this very moment? You can't. Whatever you surmise is only that, a guess. There is no way for you to know what has happened to the last meal you have eaten, whether it has already been digested, if it is still in the stomach, or where in the intestine it may be now.

You cannot know what is going on, simply because there are no instruments directed at the inside of your body to tell you this. You may know that your heart is beating because you can place your hand over it and feel the beat. Until you do that or some other action to bring the heart beat to the outside, it remains an activity that is hidden from you.

Why it is good that we are not aware of the body's invisible activities.

Yet, it is good that we cannot be aware of all of these activities. Can you imagine the severe disadvantage you will have if you are allowed to be aware of all the activities that are occurring in your body at any time?   You will not only be confused by problems you cannot fix, you will make matters worse by interfering with something that might never have become a full problem.

You may react in panic if you can 'see' the terrifying appearance of an invading bacterium, a task which is handled with calm reassurance by the body's defense system. You may become totally incapacitated when you realize an injury that the body's defenses will heal in the course of normal use. You may become entirely confused by the multilevel adjustments that have to be made to the circulatory system, just to carry the body from the lying to the standing or moving positions.

Can you imagine what the body constantly goes through to heal the numerous insults that the world throws at it every day? You only have to think of the healing process of a broken bone or that of a bruised skin, and then realize that this process goes on every day in some internal part of the body where the injuries are hidden from you.

Before the body's threshold has been reached for you to experience the pain of an injured ankle, there will have been small injuries that must have been inflicted on that ankle in the course of your many movements about your environment, injuries which the body heals automatically. Before the pains of an ulcer have been realized, the walls of the stomach will have been repeatedly injured, and healed by the body's defense system.

If you respond with such confused and frequently inappropriate reactions to these events when you are made aware of them, do you not see how inappropriate your reactions may be to the normal daily challenges that constantly affect the function of the body?

Muscular movement, more than a simple force of tension.

Take your muscle cells as an example. They provide you with the ability to move. That is a special function. It is so special that the same group of cells which can allow you to lift a heavy bag of groceries must also be able to let you play a coordinated game of tennis or do a delicate task such as signing your name.

What other sophisticated machine can do that? A fork lift can move a heavy crate. It, however, cannot also be used to toss a salad or pack a cartoon of eggs. In the same way, a machine designed to type a letter cannot also be expected to be used for hammering nails into a piece of wood.

This may seem to be an unnecessary argument, but do we not often expect performance from our muscles that we do not expect from other seemingly more capable instruments?

Yet, have you ever had to do a delicate task such as signing your name after doing something heavy and demanding with your muscles such as lifting a heavy crate? You may discover a phenomenon called 'post tetanic potentiation'. Your hand tremors and you cannot direct a smooth movement at your wrist. It is then that you may realize what constant adjustments are required of those cells that form the muscles, adjustments that originate from activities at the submicroscopic level to allow you the convenience of versatility almost at demand.

There are many other functions in the body which depends on an even more sophisticated balancing of activity, the blood pressure, as an example, in the vast range of movements through which we must take our bodies.

Why it is important for you to be aware of these activities.

Can you not imagine then, that with this great amount of activity that is taking place even while you sleep, there is a great chance of some small imbalance occurring in some isolated area can cause you to experience an unaccustomed pain, unexpected exhaustion, or hindered performance? Who can say that there is not, at this very moment, an imbalance of part of the defense system causing a clot to be released into the blood stream and make its way to your heart? Will it be such a surprise to have that tireless coordination of your circulation fail for one split second and cause you to faint when you stand up? Why do we always expect that these multitudes of small activities will always function so accurately that when something goes awry we are ready to condemn ourselves as weak, or to seek remedies to remove that undesired weakness?

In fact, we should learn to accept that multiple change is constantly occurring within that apparently solid entity we know as our body. We should know that so much change goes on within it that at no time is the body at the same stage of development or health as it might have been a moment earlier.   In the same way, we cannot expect a certain stage of development or a level of health for some time in the future. If it is there, we should appreciate it . We could try to influence its presence. However, we should not expect it. Yet, we do.

If only you will appreciate the amount of different conditions that must be met in order for your body to complete any function, the expression of speech, for example, you will be more tolerant of it when it fails, and more appreciative of it when it functions as you would expect.

Part III People: A Freely Mobile and Independently Generated Source of Change.

If you can accept that you cannot be aware of the subtle activities that generate physical change because of the limitations of your instruments, and if you can accept that you cannot become aware of the submicroscopic activities that generate biological change because of the added problem of their being hidden from your instruments, you are ready to consider the existence of an even less recognizable source of activity which can generate a whole host of new and unprecedented change, human thought.

People cause change too. You know that all too well. In fact, the most annoying type of change that can be imposed on you is that brought on by another person, especially one who exerts significant authority. It may be a change of opinion or allegiance from a person whose support or endorsement you need. It may be an activity directed at changing conditions within your common environment, increasing your work load, causing you to lose something you like, or to have to deal with something you do not like. It may be an activity that changes your biological health. He or she may inflict injury, or remove a necessary sustenance.

On the other hand, that person can soothe an injury, reduce work load, or provide necessary sustenance. He or she can bring support that was not there, or create an environment which is more suitable to your needs than that which you had.

Whether it is a change of a good situation into a bad one, or a bad into a good, it still is change. And if that change is caused by the action of another person interfering with the natural course of events, it is 'people' change.

Why usually you are unprepared for change caused by people.

Just think of being in a room with a group of other people. Do you know how much activity is going on? You cannot. You may presume that all attention is focussed on a common topic, be it the speaker, an event, or a task. Yet all you have is that perception. At best, you may be right for a small minority of the group.

Yet, some of those people may be thinking of any small aspect of the common environment that strikes their fancy. This can be as simple a variation as the stance of the speaker, the color of the hair of the person in front of them, a spot on the wall, or some of the vast range of other trivia. Some people's thoughts may be directed at the words the speaker may be saying, or they may be diverted by a memory stimulated by something said or suggested.

You may, yourself have experienced a situation when, although you may be following the direction of the other person's ideas intently, some phrase or description allows you to reminisce on an experience you may have had in the past. It may be the description of a town or country which reminds you of a long forgotten holiday. It may be the reference to a bank that may have reminded you that you did not mail the rent cheque that month. At these reminders, your thoughts may digress onto subjects that are totally unrelated to the discussion at hand.

Some of these people may be focussed on a discomfort within their bodies, an experience which they cannot share with anyone else. It may be as simple as a need to go to the bathroom or as complex as the concern that a pain they may have experienced in the chest can be a heart attack. They may not even be focussed on anything, preferring to lapse in a state of unawareness because of exhaustion, boredom, or the like.

Any or all of these activities may be taking place. Yet, there is no way that you can measure them, simply be aware of them, or find out where they are directed for that matter. Many researchers have used various means to guess at other people's thoughts. All of their efforts have been influenced by nothing more than pure speculation. The pallor of a person's cheek, the movement of that person's eyes, the fluctuations of that person's pulse or blood pressure, all indicate only that a change is taking place. Usually these changes are associated with the body's reactions to a pressure that has been imposed 'on it from the environment.

If there is no observable pressure from the environment, the presence of these changes may suggest that the activity which influenced these changes have come from a source which is not readily obvious, the other person's thoughts. This may be true. Then, again, we know that there are subtle activities within the material environment that are not necessarily obvious but against which the body automatically has to defend itself. Regardless of whether they arise from the person's thoughts, they still do not indicate what those thoughts may be or what may be influencing them.

Like any other change caused by an activity which you cannot measure, people's hidden thoughts can cause troublesome change. Until a person chooses to express his or her thoughts, those thoughts remain hidden within the person. When those thoughts are expressed, the change they impose is not necessarily related to other readily identifiable events.

That change can be a totally new, totally unexpected action. The thoughts are hidden, and they are generated from such a wide range of activities that no one can determine with any presumption of accuracy what may be influencing those thoughts. Since you also cannot determine what those thoughts are or how much of those thoughts, if any will be expressed by that person, it remains an indisputable fact that you never will be able to prepare yourself for the change that another person can perpetrate on you or on the common environment you share with that person.

Why you should not be exposed to all of the activities that form other people's thoughts.

Just as you are spared the limitations that can arise from being able to experience all the activities that are occurring in nature between you and the subject you wish to observe, just as you are spared the frustration that can arise if you are able to experience the activities the body must evoke in order to maintain its integrity in a changing environment, so too you are spared the immense confusion that can take place if you truly are able to experience the multifarious thoughts that people constantly activate.

One of the most delightful activities which we can enjoy as human beings is that of communicating with other people. One of the most interesting challenges in which we can indulge, and one which stimulates our most superior talents of reason and logic is that of exploring and analyzing the thoughts and intents behind an action which another person expresses. The excitement which can be elicited when you have the opportunity to learn from the ideas which another person has been able to develop from his or her experiences and extrapolate into his or her thoughts has no equal.

Just imagine how irritated and disappointed you will be to have to go through the trouble to develop some elaborate or intricate plan if everyone else will know about them before you reveal them.
Just imagine how bored you will be if you can communicate with your spouse or friend so easily that before that other person expresses himself or herself you know what he or she is about to say.
There will be no need for you to communicate with the other person. You will already be familiar with whatever that person has to say to you. He or she will no longer be a challenge or even a source of inspiration to you.

How you know that these activities exist.

Yet, you cannot know that these activities exist! Mankind has developed instruments to measure the presence of submicroscopic particles that form the elements. We have instruments to allow us to measure some of the activities that take place within the body. We even are able to measure the presence of activities that are too small or too transient by measuring the effects of their presence.

Yet, we have not been able to develop anything that measures the presence of a person's thoughts or even if that person is thinking. The nearest we have reached is to measure brain wave patterns. Still, we have not been able to associate these with the presence, absence, or degree of thought activity. However, you know that the human being thinks. You know that only because you can think yourself. You cannot conclude that the other person thinks similarly to you. You can presume it, and that is how it remains, a presumption.

There is something, however, which we have learned to associate with thought. In fact, it is this association which has allowed us to presume that the human being is the only mammal which has a highly developed intelligence, that we think. This association is the expression of creative ideas.

When a person thinks, he or she has the ability to express a solution to a problem. The result of thinking is the expression of a new idea, not just the revelation of a learned trivia or a practiced response. Any computer or tape recorder can express a range of stored information. Any dog can express a learned response without doing any more that it has been taught repeatedly. Any wild animal can do a complex task by instinct without adapting that response to the great variations that are imposed on it by the changing environment.

The human being, on the other hand, will express something which varies according to the challenge that stimulates the response. We will build a house that withstands the freezing cold of the Canadian Winter differently from how we will build a house that must protect us from the hot monsoons in India.

The Power of the unmeasurable activity of thought.

Look around you. Every man-made material, every activity that can be controlled by the human being has evolved from the activity of thought. Sure, the basic materials have always been there because mankind has never created, nor can ever create something from nothing. However, the ways that the materials have been rearranged to satisfy some useful purpose have all emanated from the activity of thought. The activity of thought may not directly affect these materials. The designs for their rearrangements, however, are the direct results of thought.

The metal that forms a motor car has always been just a piece of metal until the concepts formed by the activity of thought allows it to be transformed into an internal combustion engine. Anthropologists have observed that without such activity, all life forms remain at the mercy of the elements. Those that use only what materials are available, never shaping nor forming them, usually become extinct when those materials have been used up or when they are no longer able to help them withstand the elements.

If the activity of thought gives rise to the ability to change something else, then thought must be more powerful than that other activity. You know that the activity of the elements is a powerful activity. Therefore, thought must also be a powerful activity. Yet, not only is thought powerful, it is a tirelessly constant activity.

You cannot know when someone else is thinking. Therefore, you cannot know whether they are not thinking. You can, however, know that you are thinking. You know that you are always thinking, even when some observer may believe that you are not. Even when you are asleep, the activity of thought continues.

REM sleep, or rapid eye movement sleep has been associated with the activity of dreaming. Yet, this may pose a dichotomy. If no one can determine the activity of thought when you are awake, and if they also cannot measure it when you are asleep, how can it be presumed that REM sleep occurs when you are dreaming? This, then, can only be a presumption.

The activity of thought is so private, so personal, that it can continue tirelessly as that hidden activity until you are ready to expose it. That is a powerful force. Even the elements do not have such power. Their activities are fully exposed to the materials they can affect. They do not have the advantage of surprise. The materials they affect, therefore, have the opportunity to develop a resistance to the effects of these activities.

The activity of thought, on the other hand, does not have to be exposed until the appropriate solution has been devised. This is why we have been able to develop materials that are equal to the pressures imposed on them by the   elements and use them for some time before the elements can destroy those materials. The hidden nature of your thoughts, however, is what allows you to have the ability to gather information until you are satisfied that you can solve a problem without the disadvantage of being contradicted at each stage in the development of that solution. This is a powerful force. If you can accept that power is not only the ability to overwhelm the opposition but can also be the ability to withstand all that the opposition can throw at you, then you will accept that the activity of thought is a force of tremendous power.

Why you need people's thoughts as independent activities.

Even though people's thoughts are private, even though that privacy can cause those people to be formidable forces against you just as they are powerful forces in the environment, you need those activities. Just imagine what you will have if that activity did not occur in the people who preceded you in this world.

Not only will you be unable to enjoy the toys and instruments that are available for you to use, you will have little on which to build. If Albert Einstein did not have the benefit of Newtonian algebra or Euclidian geometry, he could not have developed the more advanced theories of relativity. If, instead, you had to experience everything personally, you would be so busy re-inventing the wheel or re-discovering fire that you would not have any time or opportunity to expand your knowledge. Therefore, the only way that you can truly increase your visions is to take into account the privately developed ideas of other people. Here, the old adage, "It is a wise man who learns even from the fool", makes good sense.

Mankind does not have a universal awareness. You are an individual, and you possess individually generated activities of thought. You share those thoughts at your personal discretion. It is this ability to develop ideas privately and share them at a certain stage of their development that has allowed mankind to be such a powerful force in this vast and formidable environment.

Why it is important to be aware of the existence of the independent activity of thought.

Great, so people think, and these thoughts are activities that are occurring privately within them, activities that will be there whether you are concerned about them or not. If that is the case, why bother to try to understand something that was there before you learned about it and which will continue to be there just as independently despite all of your attempts to understand it?

Although the activity of thought is private, the expression of that thought affects the common environment. The expression of thought, therefore is a source of change. The activity of thought is the generator of that change. Just as with change which occurs from the activity of the elements, change that comes from the expression of another person's thoughts can destroy that which you have grown to know and enjoy.

If you also can remember that when a person expresses his or her thoughts, that person is expressing a solution for a part of the vast environment which he or she sees more deeply than another (remember the power of thought is intensity, not immensity), you will appreciate that the imposed change may also be a solution for some problem which you may not have seen within that familiar environment.

By appreciating that thought, even as experienced by other people is a private, intense activity, you will be able to accept that the change they can create is not necessarily bad or dangerous. It is a different perspective on a world that is itself in a state of constant change, one which needs change in order to exist. You also will be able to accept that the only way you can get both depth and scope in your understanding of this vast and beautiful world is by fuelling your thoughts with the challenges you derive from the expressions of other people's thoughts.

Epilogue.

It is important to know how pervasive change can be, not to be neurotic about its presence, but to be aware of it. Ignorance about the presence of something does not preclude its existence. It only makes it less obvious .... to you.

This monograph, then, is intended to alert you to the depth of things that are constantly occurring so that, when the accumulated effects are presented to you, you will be better prepared to address them. It is the person who is not taken by surprise that is more capable of adjusting his or her approach to address a new situation confidently.

You do not have to examine every material for the expected deterioration, your body for every discomfort or weakness, or your associates for every change of opinion. It is sufficient only to know that these changes are natural, so that when they occur, you will know that they do not represent any personal affront to you or any indication that you have been incompetent.

You also must be aware that as much as things may change in directions that are alien to your desires, further change can take them back to their original states or into more acceptable directions. In other words, change as a continuous activity can bring more acceptable conditions as much as it can cause unacceptable ones to evolve. Remember this when dealing with the opinions and allegiances of other people, your own health, or the activities that make your tasks difficult and sometimes unrewarding.

Chapter 3.

The resources you have for dealing with change.

The human being is a singular creature. We are more than the mere mass of protoplasm that you observe to be shaped into a mobile form with limbs, muscles to move those limbs, and a brain to direct those muscles. We are thinking, creative existents with feelings and understanding.

We are able to use reason and logic to relate to the world. With the ability to think, we can plan and create solutions to new problems. We can move and shape the world in ways which seem limited only by your personal vision. We can do this along paths that are completely divergent from the natural paths. As human beings, we are able to conquer whatever new challenges the environment can throw at us, and survive them.

As an example, the human being has developed the ability to build houses to live in, adapting them to the various weather conditions we have moved ourselves to occupy. Humans have invented pots in which we cook, plates from which we eat. We have developed cars and planes to carry us over great distances, medicines to treat us, and computers and other machines to work for us. We have been able to do this without evolving into distinctly separate species. Each person has the capacity to learn to do any one of these activities or any combination of them.

On the contrary, other creatures are forced into an existence that is totally dependent on the whims of their environment. Inanimate objects react. They have an effect on the environment just by being in the path of some external activity. We do not change our environment purely by reaction.

Instinct can allow a spider to spin an intricate web. But a spider will spin a web within a predictable range in which any other member of its species will function. Instinct allows a bee to build a hive which is geometrically the most ideal for its function. But a bee does not attempt to improve on it. What a bee does is no different from what another bee of the same species will do, or has done in the past.

Instinct can allow a beaver to gnaw a tree and build a dam. Yet a beaver does not take measurements of water flow, detailed observations of high and low water marks, or comparative assessments of durability of different trees in order to keep improving her dam building techniques. She just fells the nearest tree and builds a dam. By such instinct, a beaver in northern Canada will do what a beaver in the American Midwest will do, no more, no less. We, on the other hand, do not create our effects because of instinct alone.

Some mammals which have been considered to be higher in the evolutionary scale have been observed to teach their young certain tricks of healthy survival which has been passed down each succeeding generation. Yet, after leaving home, the adult will not be much different from another adult of a previous generation, and she will teach the same to her young, and so on.

Of course, we are not saying that other species do not adapt to the demands of the environment. They certainly do. A dog, for example, will learn to respond differently from another dog of the same breed in a different home environment. The point, however, is that the dog can learn only as much as it is taught, either by the owner, or by the demands from the immediate environment. It does not create new ideas.

The Intelligent Species.

The human being thinks. Thinking is an act of creativity. It is the use of reason and logic to effect a conclusion. You know that the human being thinks because what is revealed by a person is not just a learned response to a stimulation from the environment, a predetermined conclusion, nor the reaction from blind instinct. Rather, what comes out of a human being as a result of this act of thinking is a new course of action, one which has been determined specifically for the problem which that person is addressing.

What sets you apart from other animal species is this fact - that each new generation of humans does not simply follow on the discoveries and teachings of the previous generation. Instead, as a human being, you use what you are taught only as the base from which you build new and more elaborate ideas. Look at the book you are reading. Both the ink, and the paper on which it is printed are improvements on those used in the past generation, and far more sophisticated than the parchments used, for instance, in the Dead Sea Scrolls.

It is this ability to think, this capacity for reason and logic which sets you apart from other species and defines you as homo sapiens. It is the ability to assess an unknown and to understand it, the dynamically active force which seems to become stronger the more it is used that gives you the power to deal with the demands which your changing world throws at you.

You probably are aware of present concerns about artificial intelligence and so wonder why we are making so much fuss about something which you may share with an electronic device. You must not interpret artificial intelligence, however, as being artificial reason and logic. Artificial intelligence is the ability to compare the application of new information against stored and dynamically updated patterns. As new computer chips which can do hundreds of parallel functions over one small circuit are developed, the speed of computation, and therefore the amount of considerations that will be possible over a given time, will increase dramatically. Then, choices will be made from such a large amount of new information and tested against such a large array of stored patterns that comparative decision making will probably be done more effectively by the computer than by the human.

This, however, is not the act of thinking. Thinking is more than the consideration of all the possible permutations within a fixed parameter that pertain to an existing challenge as, for instance, the movements on a chess board. It is more than the ability to choose the most appropriate response from a series of different bits of information stored from previous observations. It is the ability to originate new ideas, create new insights and explore new opportunities.

A Question of Value.

If you will recognize a very simple axiom, you will be able to understand what is, perhaps, the most important factor in the human being's search for survival.

"Something exists only as long as it remains that thing which it was in the first place. If it has been changed from its original condition, then it is something else. The original object no longer exists".

Inanimate objects have value, therefore, only if they are capable of satisfying what can be expected of them while still being those objects. This is why apparently similar objects can have very different values. An expensive oak desk has a structure that allows it to function as a useful desk longer than, say, a cheap imitation made from particle board.

The value of some other things can be determined by parameters that are less stable. For example, the value of an explosive charge is not related to how stable it is as much as its degree of instability. The underlying inference is that the value of anything is determined by how well it is able to satisfy the expectations placed on it.

You, however, have a value because of what you can do, what you can contribute to this world. One thing that you and everyone else hold true about ourselves is that we are individuals. You are not just the object you appear to be. Unlike the inanimate object, you have no value just by being. Your value is not measured by how long you can remain intact as a visible object without being destroyed.

Look around. Every human being has what you seem to have have, two arms, two legs, a torso. Yet, they are just tools which each person develops to different levels of usefulness. Some people cannot use them at all. Some people have shaplier bodies, prettier faces, longer legs. Yet, as you know, these attributes are only skin deep. A beautiful girl (or handsome man) who just sits there has little value. His or her beauty wears thin after a while. Your value is more than just being, more than just existing.

You know that you are not just that body by which you are recognized. Thank goodness for that. One thing you know about that body is that, from the time it has been conceived, it gets older, if not visibly from the outside, is does so from the inside. You do not wave good-bye to part of yourself whenever you flush the toilet. You do not reduce yourself as a person whenever you clip your nails and throw the clippings into the garbage. As a human being, you are more than the physical body. You are a thinking, creative mind.

It is you, the mind which makes you unique. It is you, the mind which makes you the individual, even in a community of homogeneous people, even next to your identical twin. It is you the mind which grows and becomes stronger while the physical body deteriorates through its limited life span.

A search for Identity.

You do not get up in the morning and check with the mirror to determine if the person who is there is really you. You know that it is you. If, when you check in the mirror, you see a body which you do not recognize as the one you had the day before, your reaction will not be, "Who is this person?". Rather, you will wonder what happened to your body. You know yourself, not by your body, but by your awareness, that mind.

It is logical to assume that if something seems to function along divided paths as the human person seems to do, that thing must be composed of two entirely independent parts. One fact you know about yourself is that you were born without the range of insight and awareness you have now. The mind becomes stronger as you grow.

Another thing you know is that, even if your body has become bigger and stronger since birth, the tissues of an adult will have become older and less resilient than those of a child. Each attribute seems to be moving in independently opposite directions, one getting more powerful while the other gets weaker. They must, therefore, be two distinct entities.

You also will recognize that there are times when you are physically exhausted while being in high spirits mentally as, for example, after winning a strenuous game, and that even if you are physically rested, when you receive depressing news, you still will become mentally distressed. Can this happen if one state is a function of the other? If so, would not the hormone or chemical that produces the mental effect be as exhausted as the rest of the body? Would it not also be as recharged as other chemicals would be when the body is rested?

If these identities function so independently, they will have to be two independently distinct entities, wouldn't they?   If you have chosen to protect or promote one in preference to the other, or to push the other when they both are exhausted, you will have established, not only that you recognize their distinct natures, but that you identify with one over the other, will you not?

In the case of the human condition, you will find that it is easier to push yourself to do something if you are physically exhausted but mentally refreshed than you can if you are mentally depressed but physically rested. You also will recognize that if you are both physically exhausted and mentally depressed, you will be more inclined to seek help for your mental state in preference to your physical state if only one can be addressed.

We must conclude then, that you are not a body with a mind. You do not have a mind. If, too, the soul is that part of the human existence which is not visible on the outside and which promotes the person to being a superior species, that entity which we also refer to as the mind, we also can say that you do not have a soul. Rather, you are a soul, or a mind. You have a body.

That is why you compete. That is why you push yourself to show that you can accomplish a goal, even when it hurts your body. It is because you are not the body. You are a mind. You use the body.

The human dilemma.

We have seen that the value of any object is its ability to be useful within its limitations, or better yet, to be able to exceed those limitations. We have seen that the human being is more than just a blob of flesh. You are a mind. You can think. Therefore, your value must be related to that specific function. You already know that. Whether you have expressed it or not, your main desire is to be respected for the contribution of your mind, not just for your body.

Inanimate objects and other life forms can function comfortably within defined limitations. A flower, therefore, is a complete flower if it blooms, produces pollen, and is able to turn toward the sun. A worker bee has fulfilled its purpose if it gathers nectar, a spider if it spins a web like that of other spiders of the same species. Even the ape and dolphin, species that are considered to be more intelligent than many others, by doing the simple tasks which we teach them, can demonstrate that they are able to exceed the limits which define what an ape or dolphin has evolved to be able to do. These objects and life forms, at least, by having a limit, can function contentedly within those limits.

You, on the other hand, because you are an invisible mind, have no measurable limits to tell you that you have reached your fullest potential. Because that mind is a growing entity which can be as great as you train it to be, there is no fixed parameter which can tell you that whatever you have achieved is the peak of your potential. Regardless of what you may have achieved, you always will be haunted by the belief that you can do better, that what you have done is not good enough.

One of the greatest minds of science, Sir Isaac Newton may shed some light on this frustration of the human being. This is even more relevant when we consider that Sir Isaac Newton was acknowledged in some circles as having almost supreme intelligence that he was often exemplified as the second coming of Christ. We may think that he would grow to be arrogant with that distinction, but, in his more humble private writings, he says:

"I do not know what I may appear to the world; but to myself I seem to have been only like a boy playing on the seashore, and diverting myself in now and then finding a smoother pebble or a prettier shell than ordinary, while the great ocean of truth lay all undiscovered before me."

Perhaps this sentiment is more simply stated by Albert Einstein who when he was complimented by an admirer for being so much more knowledgeable than he, Albert Einstein was reported to have said,

"My friend, the difference between what you know and what I know is infinitesimal when compared with the difference between what I know and what I still do not know."

It follows, therefore, that as a human being, you are obliged to go about, forever trying to better your previous achievement, forever wondering if what you are is good enough to satisfy the expectations which you cannot define of an entity which you cannot accurately identify.

It is a sad state of affairs to discover that the species which purportedly was created to be masters of the world, to have domain over the lesser creatures, to

"Be fruitful, multiply, fill the earth and conquer it. Be masters of the fish of the sea, the birds of heaven and all living animals on earth.",

as is stated in the book of Genesis, will so frequently be unhappy, unsure about what he or she has to do, how worthwhile are his or her accomplishments.

Yet, and this is the dilemma of the human condition, the attribute which gives the human being that power, the mind, is so invisible, so inaccessible to conventional means of detection, that no one can know with any degree of certainty how capable or how great that mind has become.

The Pursuit.

Since you cannot identify that entity which you know as yourself, and since without knowing that, you cannot define a measure through which you can know when you have achieved your full potential, what you need then, is some recognition that what you are or what you have achieved is good enough to be what you should be or should achieve. You need to be accepted, to be considered, to be approved, to be respected. It is a need that permeates every person. You are no exception.

When you get that recognition, acceptance, approval or respect, you feel good. Call it ego. Call it self esteem. Call it emotions or what you will. The fact is that when you are able to display a competent profile, when the representation you make of yourself to the world is acceptable to that part of the world you are attempting to shape, or when it satisfies some authority within it, you feel good!

Feeling good is a mental experience. You do not feel good in your stomach, toe, or head. YOU feel good. That feeling is not localized to any particular part of the body. You already know that such an association cannot exist. You are not a body, not even a part of it. Therefore, what you experience is not a bodily experience. Obviously, when you do not feel good, that bad feeling or absence of good feeling is experienced, not in the body, but within you, the mind.

To be happy, to be fulfilled, to know that you are good enough to be what you were destined to be, that is your ultimate objective.

That, too, is the objective of every other person, regardless of how he or she elects to attain that objective. You offer your best ideas. You put up your best front. You improve on your presentation of yourself. All this is done in order to arrive at that state of being comfortable, being fulfilled. And you can be fulfilled only when you know that what you are is good enough to be what you should be.

Without any other measure, without any other way of knowing that you have satisfied your objective, you must rely on a measure which is as ethereal as the subject which it measures, that feeling of fulfilment. And one way you know that you can receive that feeling is through the feedback from the world, feedback of recognition, acceptance, approval, or respect.

The pursuit, then, is to be able to get recognition for what you can do or show you can do. If, to succeed at that, you must represent yourself to be strong enough to deal with the challenges that draw out the best of you, then so be it. Your immediate pursuit then becomes that of discovering the strengths you may have to allow you to make a strong representation of yourself in the issues that challenge you.

You can see the possible directions in which this can lead you. The simple equation is that, to be happy or fulfilled, what you show of yourself must be acceptable to the world or that part of it to which you show yourself. Because you are a hidden entity, what you truly are cannot be assessed by the world. What is assessed is that part of your strengths as are visible to the world.

Beauty and stamina - your most visible attributes.

The sweet, cuddly package that you were when you were born; the resemblance you had to the people who were responsible for you - your parents; the human appearance of your body; these all formed the parameters by which you first were assessed. In fact, the very first assessment was made to ensure that you, as a baby, were truly a human being. From that first observation, the assumption is made that therein lies a person. No one could ever be sure that a baby is a person until that baby starts revealing a personality of its own. Yet, the assumption is made simply on the physical, or as I prefer to refer to it, the biological appearance. Without showing any other attributes, with no indication of having something unique to offer the world other than the mere fact that it appears to be a human being, a baby is accepted as a person.

It is no small wonder, therefore, that in the first few years of your life, you see yourself as that body. You see your strengths as the strengths of that body, the skills it can express. You want to grow to be tall, fair, agile, muscular, or beautiful. With those attributes, you know that you are as strong as you can be, or at least, strong enough to be accepted by the world.

This is the most visible attribute you have. Sometimes, it is the only way through which you can identify yourself. If so, you become stuck at this level of development. You may feel powerful as long as the body continues to grow; as long as you keep it in an environment which considers it attractive; as long as it continues to function well enough for you to display a capable profile.

When it begins to weaken, maybe with age, maybe with illness, tiredness, or stress, or when you have moved to an environment which does not consider your body attractive or your skills useful, you can become lost. This, sadly, is the case with a lot of people.

Then, again, you may have allowed that strength to be enhanced by another visible identity. Sometimes, this can reduce the pressures on the body as your sole attribute. Having a respectable heritage, for example, can be the second most visible attribute you can have, next to physical strength and stamina. In fact, it frequently is the identity by which you most often describe yourself. Unfortunately, it too can be diluted by age, become less effective in unfamiliar surroundings, or become sullied or tarnished by the effects of outside influences. Then, as a result of losing this attribute, again you can become lost.

The possession of significant material wealth, as another example, can be an effective source of visible strength. A wealthy person always seem stronger than a poor person. It is not always what that person does with his or her wealth as much as the fact that he or she has them that makes that person appear strong. Perhaps, less personal than a heritage, much less so than your biological body, material possessions can still be attributes that allow you to receive the recognition, acceptance, approval, or respect you desire. Again, its power too is relative to the situation in which it is used. Great wealth can be unimportant in some circumstances, or even insignificant when the demands are too much greater.

If these are so strong that you do not have to do any more than just exist, believing that your body will always be attractive, strong, or agile, that your good name will always be respected, that your wealth will always be substantial, you can easily become complacent and allow your personal development to be retarded. If these are your attributes, is it not obvious that you are depending, for your strength, on something over which you have little control? Is it small wonder, then, that so many wars have been started because of people's fears that their bodies may be hurt, their heritage destroyed, or their wealth taken away, and with these, their own identities?

Fortunately, many people are not endowed with external strengths that are powerful enough to carry them very far. Usually, you will have discovered at an early age that these attributes had limited appeal.

It may be because you were born to a situation which demanded more of you than could be satisfied by passive beauty or specialized skills, personal heritage, or inherited wealth - for example, parents who were too busy or too drained to give much attention to you just for being there.

You may have been encouraged to venture out into the world, to a more expansive environment, one that was not easily impressed by your basic appearance, one that did not respect you by your heritage, or one that was not impressed by the value of your wealth - for example, a highly competitive peer group, an educational system that was geared to bring out your deeper qualities, or a community that was more interested in their own attributes to give regard to yours.

It may have been because you inherited a body that was considered unattractive or one limited by some inherited or acquired malfunctions, a name that was not important or well respected, or possessions that were not considered to be of significant value.

If any of the above occurred in your development, you would have had to look deeper for more strength than you obviously had in the attribute you saw as your identity. You would have had to discover that your strengths are not limited to those things that are of value only relative to the time, the situation, or the community.

Yet, despite the distinct advantage which people can get by having to develop greater attributes than are provided by their visible strengths, it is customary to hear some people bemoaning the fact that they did not have the attributes with which another person was born. They also do not recognize that the other person frequently had to rely so totally on those attributes that he or she may not have developed any other attributes, only to be caught thoroughly unprepared when these visible attributes are discovered to be fragile.

It is only when you discover that your physical beauty, skill, and stamina may no longer be effective as attributes, when the advantage which you may have had with your heritage dies with those who know its background, and when your wealth no longer gives you the strength to stun the opposition that you will recognize the limitations inherent in those attributes that are visible. The more visible they are, the more easily they can be destroyed.

It is only then that you will become motivated to look deeper, and discover more personal attributes. This can happen in your early development if you were given the opportunity to expand your personal attributes. It can happen later in life if you had had the privilege of applying your more visible attributes successfully and then seeing them fail.

Insight and understanding, your deeper, more personal attributes.

When what you appear to be is not good enough to satisfy the world or that part of it to which you are exposed, you have little choice but to find some other attribute, one that is more personally yours, to provide you with the means to regain that feeling of worth. You look deeply within yourself for strength that is more useful, more applicable than that which has been rejected as insufficient, there being no other alternative. When you do so, you discover that you have experience in some areas which other people have difficulty managing. Because of your experience, these particular challenges may seem easy for you - easy to understand, and easy to manage. That experience has allowed you to 'see' those areas of your world more clearly than is visible to the casual observer. You now have discovered that you have insight and understanding.

The insight you have into these challenges and the understanding you have for their management become new attributes which define you more specifically than you were defined by the more visible attributes with which you were endowed. You now have attributes that are personally yours.

You now have something to offer to the world, something which is more than just what you were given. Like the servant described in the parable of the ten talents, you are able to display more than you were given. Suddenly, you have a unique attribute. You have insight, and the understanding which that insight brings, an attribute you can display to impress your world with your prowess. Sometimes it becomes all that you need to satisfy their expectations and earn for yourself the affirmation that comes when what you are is good enough to be what you can be.

If so, you may become stuck at this level of development. You may feel powerful as long as what you know, or what you can show that you know, continues to be greater than what is expected of you; as long as you stay in an environment which expects no more of you than that understanding. Sometimes, that insight or understanding may be so powerful in a particular area as, for example, the ability to do a specialized task or play a particular game well, or the ability to compute a certain level of mathematics or remember a certain amount of trivia, that you receive full recognition for what you already have and lose all incentive to get more.

Fortunately, many people are not endowed with such insight that they are able to go very far without improving it. A more skilful player can make the previously successful athlete look unimpressive. A new wave of trivia can make the information possessed by the most widely read person redundant. New discoveries in the field of science for example, can cause any person's limited knowledge to be obsolete. A new twist to an old problem can make the previous solution redundant.

It is a tempting, and very frequently used defense to avoid such fall from grace by staying within those situations that do not grow more demanding. Then some people can be allowed the 'privilege' of not having a more capable athlete to show them up. They may never be allowed to be exposed to situations where the trivia they know is obsolete. They may be brought up in such protected environments that they are not challenged by any but the most compatible interpersonal relationships. They may always appear successful and powerful. But they will have lost the opportunity to look deeper, to discover attributes that are even stronger than the personal insights and understanding.

If you have had the good fortune of being challenged to the limits of your personal insight and understanding, you will have learned that, no matter how strong they are, these attributes have limitations. They are 'linear', so to speak, in their growth. You may, for example, spend the time and energy gathering insight in the field of medicine. You cannot, at the same time, gather insight in the field of literature. Given the overlap that is inherent in any field, you still will appreciate the limitations that your insight and understanding has.

It is only when your insight and understanding have been challenged beyond the level to which you have developed them that you will get the opportunity to search for deeper attributes. You will discover that every time you find a deeper attribute, it is something unripe, something you have to take nurture into a useful talent. You have to develop it.

Reason and logic - your most flexible attribute.

When the understanding and insight you have is insufficient to satisfy the demands of some part of your world, you again lose the feedback affirmation that what you are is good enough to be what you can be. The need to feel good, to feel fulfilled, still is paramount in you as in everyone else. And, if to restore that good feeling, you must have more of that insight and understanding, or, at the least, insight that is appropriate to the situation you must manage, you have little choice but to go to its source. Wherever you acquired it in the first place must be able to supply you with more.

This may seem, on the surface, to be a superfluous argument. You may see insight and understanding as possessions the human being acquires automatically. That may be so. If, however, you need something in greater quantity or at a faster rate than is automatically available, it becomes necessary for you to approach the source and influence its supply. With that in mind, you examine the possible sources.

One possibility is that you may have been born with knowledge that matures as you grow. Another is that you were endowed with genes that predetermined the insight or potential for insight that you have. Please do not dismiss these as unnecessary considerations. The original purpose for I.Q. tests was to show that children of the upper classes were better endowed with intelligence that were children of the lower classes. A third possibility is that the insight and understanding you have were provided by the teachers and mentors who trained you.

You know that you were not born with the insight you have now, or with what you had at any stage of your development. In fact, you know that you are much more knowledgeable, more insightful now than you were yesterday, and even more so than you were as a child.

You know that your insight and understanding did not develop automatically with the maturing of your body or the evolution of your genes. If that was the case, you would have acquired as much insight if you were locked up in your parent's attic for your whole youth as you did being as exposed as you were to the world.

You know that it did not come from the food you ate. But, you do know that it had something to do with the training you had, whether it was given by your parents, friends, or traditional teachers at school. Yet, if you think about it, you will realize that you had about the same training as did your twin, if you have one, or as much as the kid who sat next to you at classes.

What this points out is that these teachers provided only challenges. In some cases, they may have broken down the challenges into smaller 'chewable' sizes. This is what differentiates a good teacher from a poor one, only how he or she can break down the problem for you to solve, and how quickly he or she will proceed to the next level.

The twenty children in a class who received the same instruction and who were given the same challenges did not develop the same insight and understanding. One factor to be considered is the attention each one paid to the information. Each person will develop insight on what he or she has been considering, whether it is the face of the girl in the next seat or the dream of making a great play in the next football game. What this reveals is that what insight you acquire is dependent on how you decide to direct your thoughts.

In the same way, the person who takes the information from the teacher and works on it will develop greater insight into the subject than the person who simply listens in class and does no further studies. Is it not logical, therefore, that you are the source of your own insight and understanding? Whatever you have, you put it there. You have no one to thank but yourself. You have no one to depend on but yourself.

Yes, it frequently is helpful to receive some of another person's understanding of an issue for you to be able to understand it more thoroughly. Yet, even that understanding is not simply transferred from the other person to you. Whatever you understand must be derived from your reason and logic, your ability to create a personal understanding from the information available. Whenever that other person makes a contribution from his or her understanding, it becomes information. It is understanding and insight only within you, after you think on it and create the insight that is personal to the way you see it.

You, therefore, are the source. You are the thought-energy, the source of reason and logic which provides the insight and understanding with which you represent yourself to the world as a person with a contribution that is unique to you and applicable to those parts of the world to which you have been exposed.

'Reason and logic' is an activity. The activity is the act of thinking, the act of creativity. By using it, you will have 'created' new attributes, those which you did not have before you created them. This, therefore, is no longer a linear attribute. It is completely flexible.

It is not a possession which has limits to its applications. You can think on anything. In fact, unlike your more visible attributes, or even those which you can make visible by choice, your insight and understanding, creativity is useful when you are challenged by things that are beyond your developed attributes. You now have determined the source, the generator of useable attributes, you - the thought-energy within that body.

As that source of thought energy, you must need two things for you to function to your full potential. One of these is the challenge that stimulates you. The other is the fuel you need to feed that energy.

The first is easy. The challenges are available from the world. They are the problems that are beyond your developed attributes. What you do not understand, what is beyond the vision of your developed insight, these are the challenges which stimulate your act of creativity. But, creativity does not always function at its peak. There are times when you are more creative than others.

Creativity, also, is not always challenged. Sometimes, as with your other attributes, you may erroneously have been provided with a stable environment, one which does not require that you create any more understanding and insight than you already have acquired. Then you will have lost out on developing the single resource which makes you into a unique person, a competent human being.

If, however, you have had those challenges, you will have real-ized that, to stimulate that thought-energy, you needed something else, the fuel that energizes it. Again, you need to find a source, but now it is a source of energy that stimulates your creative activity and gives it efficiency.

Your major liability - the need for affirmation.

When you feel good, you can think. When you are depressed, when you are unfulfilled, you cannot think creatively. This is not an axiom. It only is an observation which you can make about yourself. It has less to do with the state of your physical body than it does with your mental state.

We have come to the final source, the energy to fuel the generator that gives you more of the attributes that make you into a competent human being. Where do you get it? Do you remember the "feeling good feeling" that you get when you know that what you are is as good as what you can be? That is the energy, the inner strength which fuels your creativity. You get it from the recognition, accep-tance, approval, or respect through which the world affirms you as a competent human being.

This presents a dilemma. It seems that the energy you need to al-low you to develop the attributes to be strong enough to deal with the challenges of the world comes to you when you are able to sat-isfy the demands which the world places on you. You seem to be able to get affirmation when you do not need it and you do not get it when you do need it.

This dependence on the world for the affirmation to fuel your creativity is your liability. You have some control over every other attribute you possess. Yet, the one factor that allows you to build on those attributes, your creativity, seems to be controlled by out-side forces, and these forces seem reluctant to give you what you need.

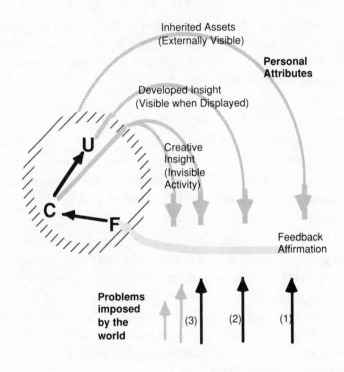

C = CREATIVITY **U** = UNDERSTANDING **F** =FULFILMENT

Problem level (1) - Set of problems that can be managed with visible assets

Problem level (2) - Set of problems that can be managed with developed
           insight and understanding

Problem level (3) - Set of problems that can be managed with
           creative insight and understanding

Figure 1. The Affirmation Cycle

True, the world may have been willing to give it to you when you were a child. Then, when you attempted to do a task, the world may have seemed willing to compliment you on that small part which you did well. When, as an adult, you do the same task, the world seems to see only that small part which you may not have done as well as you did the larger part. Just think of how you respond to a child playing soccer and how different that response is if the player is an adult, and you will identify with the comparison.

Yet, there is one obvious method by which you can overcome that liability and get the affirmation while also getting the challenges that will stimulate your creativity. In the world, the way we want to see it, growth occurs in steps. There is a riser, followed by a plateau, followed by another riser. After each challenge, there is, or should be a period of rest, a period when you can savour your successes and recharge your energies for the next challenge. Then, by the time you are required to reach deeper to create new insight and understanding for a new problem, you have the fuel with which to do so. You get mileage from the attributes you have acquired to date. But, you know that, in reality, this is not always available.

Epilogue.

If only you do not need that affirmation from a world which does not seem to want to give it, if only you can make it so secure that the only thing you seek from the world is what it truly is prepared to give you, new problems for you to solve, you will be more capable of being effective and efficient as a responsible person.

It is the intent of this work to show you how to to secure that affirmation. If you are to be the responsible person you want to continue to be, you will be the person who is expected to give affirmation to the world, not receive it from the world. You, therefore, must have a source of affirmation which is secure despite the fact that, by virtue of your own progress, you will be faced with expanding problems that dilute the effect of any affirmation you may have received.

Do not be disheartened by the discovery that the more you try to manage your challenges the more of them there are for you to manage. This is a reality of the world. You who have shown that you can take charge and deal with what is thrown at you will always be challenged by greater problems even if it is just to know where your limits are.

The capacity of the world is infinite. You do not have infinite physical strength. You do not have infinite insight. You do have, however, the creativity that will continue to work for you as long as you have the fuel to feed it. For you who have discovered your creativity, your main goal now is to discover how to assure yourself of the fuel you need to be able to use it to its fullest potential.

Chapter 4.

The Effects of modern change on creativity.

We have seen that the world is rough. We have seen that, as a human being, you have attributes that must be developed before they can be useful to you in dealing with this rough world. We also have seen that your ability to develop those attributes is nurtured by the recognition of those you already have accumulated. In other words, you are rewarded for your resourcefulness through showing what that resourcefulness has allowed you to accomplish.

This may seems to be an unfair arrangement. Yet, you are a human being. As such, you are not just a passive existent. You are a thought-energy. Therefore, it is natural that any recognition you receive must come from your ability to show that you are such a thought-energy. When you have more attributes than those you were given at the start, attributes that show you to be the individual, the existent which can see the world from a unique perspective and develop similarly unique solutions to offer to the world or some part of it, you will have earned the right to be recognized as a person of value, an important human being.

The Secure Reality.

On the surface, there seems to be a built-in paradox to this feedback system, one which allows you to get the strength you need to be creative only after you already have been creative and can show the effects of that creativity. Yet, there is no conflict. You see, you start your life with attributes that are already there for you. It is required only that you add to them.

This requisite has been ideally depicted in the parable about the three servants who each were given some money when their master went away, and who were expected to show that they had the resourcefulness to increase their assets. The first, given five talents, invested it and made five more. The second, given two talents, invested it and made two more. The third, given one talent, buried it and offered no more to the master when he returned. Recognition was given only to those who showed that they were able and willing to expand on what they were given.

In the same way, you are born with attributes that give you a start. As a human being, you have attributes in your appearance, physical strength and stamina, and in your heritage. These attributes were given to you. You cannot take credit for having them any more than you can take the blame for inheriting a handicap. Like the servants in the parable, you too are not equipped with the same amount of attributes as any other person. You may have more. You may have less. The important comparison, however, is that you have as much capability for improving those attributes as does the other person.

You also live in a system that has been designed to provide you with demands that expand progressively from those that accept your more visible attributes to those which demand more of the personalized attributes you have developed. There always is the necessity, therefore, to approach new situations from a secure and expanding home base. You have such a home base. It may be a person who likes you, a place where you can be accepted as you are, or a position which is comfortable and relaxing.

This is your **secure reality**.   When you are with those people, when you go to those places, when you are so relaxed that you know that what you are is good enough to be what you are expected to be in these conditions, you are fulfilled.

In your secure reality, you are a strong, confident person. You become fulfilled, a fulfilment which recharges you with sufficient energy to allow you to go to the next challenge and create the insight to understand, accept, and manage it. Then, your secure reality will have been expanded.

If you will look into your past, you will discover that you have enjoyed such expansion. There are many situations, tasks, and people that are part of your secure reality now, but which were frightening or uncomfortable when you were younger. These things did not become different. Riding a bicycle, for example, is no different from the challenge that seemed so formidable when you were young. Now it may be part of your secure reality. But, it was not always so. The secure reality you have now is larger than the secure reality you may have had at an earlier age.

The Insecure Reality.

Just as the things and people you enjoy now were not always a source of comfort or joy to you but have become so, so too you must realize that there are things and people which challenge or reject you now but which can become part of your secure reality some time in the future. You need only to create an understanding of them and apply that understanding in your association with them.

It is natural to assume, therefore, that under normal conditions, the nurturing you receive in a secure reality gives you enough strength to address another segment of territory, conquer it, and use your familiarity with it to expand the areas in which you feel secure.

This other segment of your environment does not give you nourishment. The attributes you have do not impress the people in this segment, nor are they able to conquer the situations. Under these conditions, your position may be uncomfortable. The people may not like you. The situations may be frightening. You are not lost, lonely, or incompetent. You only are in an **insecure reality**.

If you can accept the changes that are occurring in the minds of the people who are nearest and dearest to you, if you will consider the changes that are occurring, even now, in the materials that form your most prized possessions, if you can visualize the gradual process of aging that will accumulate to engulf your whole body, you will recognize that, regardless of how large your secure reality may be, you always will be challenged by conditions that are part of a more immense insecure reality.

In your insecure reality, you are weak. You may be afraid. Not only are you not fulfilled, you cannot get fulfilment until you can get out of that insecure reality, or conquer it. You may see, therefore, that there is no such thing as an insecure person, or even a secure person. There only is a person who, under certain conditions, is in a secure reality, and under other conditions, is in an insecure reality.

When you feel weak or frightened, you are not just an insecure person. You are a person who is functioning, at that moment, in an insecure reality. When you feel strong and confident, do not be fooled into thinking that you are a strong, confident person. You must realize that you are a person who, at that moment, is functioning in a secure reality. Activities are occurring beyond your immediate vision that will bring new situations to you. These new situations have a greater possibility of being part of your insecure reality than they have of being part of your less extensive secure reality. Then, that strength and confidence will again be reduced, determined less by you than by the depth of understanding you have for that new reality.

An insecure reality, therefore, is something which pervasively afflicts everybody. Everybody is ill at ease in an insecure reality.

The strong person is not the one who always seem strong and confident. He or she is the one who starts off with the uncertainty of an
insecure reality, is able to assess the conditions, understand them,
and then manage them as though they always were part of a secure
reality. It is how you make an insecure reality into a secure one
that determines your capability, not how well you enjoy a secure reality.

The Feedback Cycle.

Obviously, if as a human being, you are expected to be a thought-
energy, the two most important prerequisites for you to function
competently are the challenges on which you can be creative and
the inner strength with which you will fuel your creativity. We
have seen that there is no shortage of situations which can challenge your creativity. There also is an adequate supply of situations
through which you can obtain the strength to fuel that creativity.
.There is a dichotomy, however, in that each situation is the antago-
nist of the other. They cannot exist simultaneously.

You cannot be in both a secure reality and an insecure reality at
the same time. Since you need the effects of both of them for you
to be successful, there must be a way of storing one to have.it when
you address the other, and there is such. The fulfilment you get
when you are in a secure reality stays with you long enough for you
to use it in a subsequent insecure reality. Similarly, the challenge
you have from an insecure reality still is there for you after you return from being restored in your secure reality.

Such a feedback cycle is automatic and inevitable in the evolution
of your maturity. You will discover that you work more successfully and efficiently at a difficult task after you have been reassured by
your successes in others. When you have done a good and efficient
job, it is easier to go to the next task, even if you may be physically
tired.

This is the feedback cycle. You are replenished by the recognition of a past success and you approach the next problem with strength and confidence.   Obviously, staying in a secure reality may continue to give you the fulfilment you enjoy, but you will not have the stimulation of the challenges from the insecure reality. Then, your creativity will be shut down and you will not give account of yourself as a human being. Similarly, staying in an insecure reality will provide you with the challenges, but you will not have the inner strength to fuel your creativity. The net result is that you also will not be able to give account of yourself as a human being.

You need the balanced input from both. And if you cannot get them together, you will have to use them separately and in sequence, one after the other. Obviously, since the act of creativity depletes your fuel reserves, when you are attempting to manage conditions in an insecure reality, you must be able, either to return to a secure reality to restore your strength, or to make that situation into a secure reality and use it as a new source of fulfilment.

This is the whole purpose of your existence as a human being. You are designed to be able to offer solutions that are unique and specific for each challenge. To do so, you first must create understanding. You may express that understanding in order to manage a situation which you have conquered. But, even if you do not express that understanding, you still will have created it. You will have given account of yourself as a human being, an existent which has the ability to offer solutions for challenges which once were beyond you.

The Prerequisite for feedback.

When you feel good, when you are fulfilled, the strong, confident feeling, the inner strength, lasts, not only while you are in the situation that allows you to be fulfilled, it lasts even beyond it. When you are challenged by new or unknown conditions in an insecure reality, you use that fulfilment you are able to take with you as the

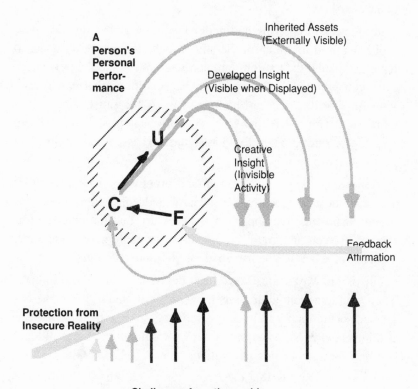

Figure 2. THE FEEDBACK CYCLE

fuel to explore the unknown and understand it. The stored fuel becomes used up.

In the act of exploring and understanding the new situation, you will have used up much of the stored fuel. If you are fortunate to have completed the exploration, and you understand the new situation, you will have re-established the conditions that can restore your fulfilment. You will be able to enjoy the satisfaction that is associated with the recognition of your accomplishment. Then, you can be strong again to address the next issue and explore the next unknown.

Obviously, this positive growth and progression cannot occur if you are not able to complete the task and enjoy the pleasure of accomplishment. Obviously, it is necessary that the challenge of the task is such that you can complete your exploration and understanding of it before you use up all of your inner strength.

This is the way it must have been devised. You get reinforced. Then you approach an unknown, overcome it, and use it as the expanded secure reality to be reinforced again for the next challenge. If things always happened this way, we would all be successful and fulfilled without needing instructions on how to become so.

The prerequisite is that each new challenge must be within the range of the inner strength you can receive from your accumulated secure reality. I suppose that it is comparable to having a bank account. You can spend as much as you have saved, the more money you have in the account, the more you have available for you to spend.

In an extension to the same comparison, you will observe that as your secure reality expands, so too will the fulfilment you receive from the expanded version. In effect, there may be a chance that the fulfilment you can receive may increase exponentially - the more you accomplish, the more areas there are from which you can be replenished and the more strength you get for accomplishing the next challenge. Then, under such circumstances, it will be easy for lenges arrive in progressively expanding stages of difficulty.

This is the way it was when the world was young. This is the way it was when you were a child. When the world was young, you would have lived in very simple surroundings. The challenges you had to face were those challenges that were relevant to your immediate society. What happened a hundred miles away did not concern you, did not affect you, and might never have been brought to your attention. You had the time to savor your successes before you were required to manage another problem. You also were reassured that you did not have to be concerned about certain problems that were presented to you. They were thought to be the specific activities of the Deity.

As a child, even in modern times, you would not have been required to solve the type of problems that are imposed on you as an adult. You would have been given the privilege of having challenges that were controlled so that they did not overwhelm you and deplete the inner strength which you had for managing them.

The reality of modern change.

This ideal progression, however, is not the way life seems to evolve. Under modern conditions, you rarely are able to savour your successes and gather enough strength to tackle the next problem. What seems to happen instead, is either that the next challenge is so large that you deplete the strength you were able to gather from your accumulated secure reality before succeeding in managing it, or that new ones come so frequently that you rarely have the opportunity to replenish yourself before having to tackle yet another problem.

What I want you to visualize again is that bank account. If what you have is enough to allow you an investment which, when mature, will pay you handsome dividends, you will be able to put back into the account more money than you withdrew. Then, you will have more to invest at the next opportunity.

If, however, the demands of the new investment is such that you deplete what you have withdrawn before you can service the investment properly, you will lose what you have invested and your account will be deficient when you want to use it next.

What this means is that, no matter how extensive are your attributes, they are limited, and can be exhausted by the demands of new or extensive problems. No matter how great your inner strength may be, it too is limited by the size, stability, and availability of your secure reality, and can be depleted by demands that are too persistent or too extensive. Simply stated, you do not have to be inadequate as a person for you to fall victim to the demands that can exhaust you. You can be just as easily overwhelmed if the demands arrive in a too rapid succession or present in a too extensive fashion.

In our modern world, there are very few people whose exposure can be so limited that everything will inundate them. The stresses of our modern world, however, can make the knowledge of the most educated person redundant.

Just as you will stagnate in barren conditions even if you have all the desire but there is nothing for you to discover, so too will you stagnate in fertile conditions if the fertility is so demanding that it exhausts the inner strength you need to fuel your creativity. The net result is that you are forced to try to deal with never ending challenges without the strength which you need for dealing with them.

The problem with modern conditions is that they are fast paced and extremely demanding. Each new challenge, therefore, has the potential to exhaust the inner strength which you have for dealing with it, and frequently it does exhaust that strength. The only way you can be sure of staying ahead seems to be for you to be infinitely knowledgeable and be sure that everything is within your secure reality, or have an unending supply of inner strength.

No one can be infinitely knowledgeable. In addition, the dichotomy in the feedback system ensures that the supply of inner strength is determined by the strength of a secure reality which, in turn, is affected by the size of the insecure reality. In a world which changes as rapidly and with such immense parameters as that which you now are experiencing, the size of your insecure reality is infinite. Then, regardless of how well established your secure reality may be, it still can be insignificant by comparison.

Modern change - why it is so demanding.

Life, as we know it, has always been affected by the same volatile environment, the same fragility of the organic body, and the same unpredictable dynamism of other people's thoughts and actions. Your insecure reality, then, must not be any greater than it would have been in more stable times. Yet the pressures of change have never been as great then as they are in modern times.

If you were to look at change within the parameters in which we described it during the discourse in chapter 2, you will understand that there couldn't be any more activity within the materials that form your physical environment than within those that formed the physical environment of your ancestors.

We may have more stable chemical structures forming fabrics that erode more slowly, but we did not get these materials from another universe. They were part of the environment before we used them. Before Marconi sent the first radio waves across the Atlantic ocean, radio waves were present.

Marconi only learned how to 'influence' the activities of an already existing phenomenon. Before we polluted our oceans with oil spills, oil was already in the earth. Mankind only relocated it.

Similarly, there could not be any more activity within your body than there was in the body of a human being one thousand years ago. We have evolved, but our evolution has not been a physical evolution of the make-up of the body.

We may have better medicines and more balanced diets than before. But medicines are not generated from nothing. They simply are the re-structuring of new chemicals or the purification and concentration of those that have always been here.

Other people's thoughts, too, are not any more diverse than they would have been in those times. They are no more or no less measurable now, than they were then. They may be influenced by things that are more modern, and perhaps, more clearly defined, or perhaps more diverse than they were back then. But, these thoughts are not any more active than were the thoughts of earlier people.

We may have languages that are more universal than the small dialects from which they evolved. But language still does not represent thought accurately. There are many instances when a person will express an idea using a string of words that accurately describe the idea, only to be misinterpreted by an observer who uses that same string of words to describe a totally different idea just as accurately.

What this all shows is that the activity was always there. Some of it has been brought to you. You have been taken to others. What makes the difference is that, even though you are exposed to more of these sources of change than you would have had to face in less volatile times, you need no greater preparation to face any of them now than you would have needed if you had to face them then.

The result of all of this is that, even though the world is not any more volatile than it ever was, you are exposed to more of the normal amount of change than you ever were, and, therefore, are more susceptible to being drained by the greater demands placed on you. What brings this about are the compounded effects of industrialization, urbanization, transportation, and communication.

Industrialization.

Mankind has always been one step behind nature. Mankind has always been able to see only as far as our instruments allowed us to see. Therefore, when we were able to invent instruments that allowed us to do more than we were able to do before, those new instruments also showed us more things that had to be done.

Just think, if you were able to plow an acre of land with a horse drawn plow, with the help of a tractor, you would be able to consider plowing ten acres, and, most surely, you would attempt it. In more modern terms, you may remember that the computer was introduced to the business world in order to save time and effort doing a lot of paper work.

In theory, bookkeepers would be able to finish their chores and have time for more creative ventures. In practice, more paper work was created by computers which gave us the ability to see more deeply into the figures and to calculate them more accurately. Typists were supposed to be more efficient because they could correct errors without having to re-type the whole thing. In practice, what was seen was the ability to create an even more stylish finish to the letter. More work and higher expectations were all that were accomplished.

Industrialization has been able to bring more of the changing world to people who, without such instruments, would never have had to experience many of the demands they are expected to address. In modern times, we are aware of the power we can get with such instruments. We sometimes let that get in the way of reason and believe that we can solve everything with the use of more powerful instruments, only to be inundated a delayed time period later with the greater problems that these more sophisticated instruments tend to reveal.

Urbanization.

The limitations which people once experienced allowed the formation of very isolated communities. People segmented themselves into groups based on the areas of the environment that were familiar to them and on the challenges it provided to their particular skills. There evolved a homogeneity among those who shared each isolated area. Their learned responses would have been influenced by the limited challenges that were common to their specific areas and the thought activities that were developed to address these limited challenges.

With industrialization, people from varied and distinct communities, attracted to the promises of greater success with the tools of industry, moved to live in newer and larger centers with other people from entirely different communities. This introduced each person to a greater variety of new ideas, personal idiosyncrasies, and deeply ingrained beliefs than they could have been prepared to address.

The other people with almost irreconcilable differences always existed. Urbanization only brought them together. In addition, urbanization attracts a more sophisticated industrialization which, in turn, serves to attract an even more diverse range of people to each urban center. Modern urbanization, therefore, brings an even greater range of people with an even greater range of backgrounds, ideas, and learned behaviours to affect each other.

Look around you now. The people sharing your office, living next door to you, or even sharing your home are highly likely to have been brought up under totally different circumstances than you were. The personal skills these other people developed to help them survive the conditions within their specific communities are almost predictably different from the personal skills you needed and developed to deal with the conditions within your specific community.

In ancient times too, a well defined class structure was established so that, even within small communities, the people with whom you related were less diverse. With industrialization came the emergence of the middle class and a greater range of backgrounds, ideas, and beliefs. It came, not only from the merging of different communities, but also from the merging of different class structures.

Transportation.

You have fast cars now to take you over a wider expanse of the environment than ever before. Aeroplanes make the farthest corner of the globe accessible within a very short time frame. In one day, it is possible for you to move from one time zone to another or from one season to another, being able to experience the full range of environmental activities that people of more ancient times did not have to experience.

There was a time when all you had to worry about were the problems that could arise within a very limited area of the common environment. That did not mean that there were not weather systems destroying crops and threatening lives in other places while your environment was safe. It does not mean that you are exposed to a more volatile environment now. It only means that, with better transportation, your immediate environment is now much more extensive than it ever has been.

Just think about it now. The range of environment which a person would expect to cover in a day, say two hundred years ago, is much less than you would expect to cover in one hour. If you drive to one store to get something which is not available there, you will think nothing of proceeding to another store much further away and expect to be able to purchase it and still return to use it that day. The distances which some people must travel to go to work and still expect to do household chores when they return may have been considered to be a week's journey in ancient times.

Communication.

Less than fifty years ago, in the mid nineteen hundreds, an important event happening in another country or some distance away in the same country would not be known for many days. News had to be brought by way of aeroplane, surface mail, or transmitted electrically through the use of a Wirephoto, the facsimile taking some minutes or even hours to be reproduced.

An event occurring in a distant place may not have affected you then. By the time you may have heard about it, much of it may have been defused. The difficulty with which such news was carried made it impossible to cover too much of the global scene. Many things would have occurred without many people in different parts of the world becoming aware of them.

Now, communication is instant. As I write this, I can use a modem and transmit the material instantly to another computer in another country. The whole world is brought to you in your living room every night as quickly as new events unfold. It now is so easy to transmit news and pictures of such events that more of them are brought to you than would have been considered important fifty years ago.

What this means is that, in modern times, you are affected by the events that occur in every corner of the globe and by the behaviours of the whole range of people that occupy that enormous environment, even if they are not important. You are required to consider more information from a wider range of sources in one day now than anyone would have had to process in a month in earlier times.

The effects of modern change on the acquisition of feedback.

When you were a child, even in this modern and rapidly changing world, you did not have to worry about the problems that were beyond those you had to address. Even consequences to your actions were diluted by the adults in your world. A spanking, for example, intended to discourage you from playing in the streets, might have been uncomfortable. Yet, it would have been a diluted consequence from the more serious possibility of being struck by a car.

You are an adult now. In our rapidly changing world, there are few precedents to guide you through the new problems that arise. There are so few people who are ahead of you, as parents are to a child, that you cannot look to them for guidance in these unpredictable times or for assistance in diluting your consequences. Now

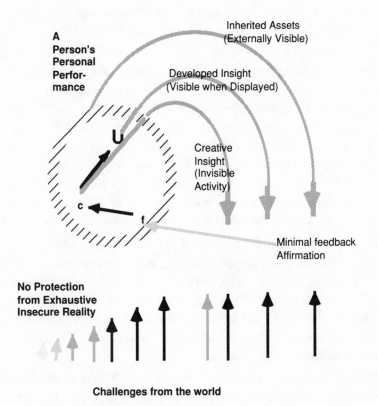

Figure 3. THE REALITY

Too many problems presented too close together causes everything
to be part of the insecure reality. The immensity causes exhaustion of
inner strength and so of creativity, causing a vicious cycle and making
it all but impossible to break the stranglehold.

that you are an adult, you are responsible for forming your own solutions, not to problems that increase gradually, but to the sudden
presence of sometimes even devastating situations.

The objective is the same. Like everyone else now and in the
past, you want to feel fulfilled. The challenge, on the other hand, is
different. You live in a world which is so immense that, in order
for you to be fulfilled, you must be able to rise above an impossible
range of expanding problems. You must prove yourself to such a
demanding world that, no matter what you do, you rarely receive
the feedback you need to feel fulfilled and be able to rise above its
challenges. The only way to break this vicious cycle is for you to
be able to secure fulfilment without having to depend on the feedback from a world that no longer provides it.

Yet, no matter how experienced you may be, it is natural for you
to look for someone ahead of you to guide you, to provide you with
a precedent, a tool by which you can measure your success. Frequently, you measure the value of a new idea, not by how well it
addresses the issue, but by how well it compares with another idea,
one that might have been developed for a totally different set of
circumstances.

Only when you realize that the solutions which another person
can offer is based on events that occurred at a different time or
viewed from a different perspective, and therefore, are created for a
different set of conditions, can you be better prepared to deal with
the evolving events that challenge your creativity in today's environment. Only when you realize that even if that precedent was set
by you yesterday, it still is very likely to be irrelevant for the conditions of today, will you be ready to focus on the more important
challenge of honing your creativity and using it to address problems
from a position of personal strength. Only then will you be ready to
devote your attention to securing the inner strength you need to fuel
that creativity.

Epilogue.

If you can appreciate the immense and unpredictable range of the changes that constantly occur even in the apparently stable conditions you have to address, you will know that your failures are less due to your own unpreparedness than they are due to the general immensity of the challenge.

If you can appreciate the relative limitations of the attributes you have developed for dealing with those infinite problems, you will know that you must learn to rely on the more flexible resource of creativity.

If you can appreciate that, as an example of what happens in the rest of the world, even while you are formulating an answer to a question I may have asked you, I still am thinking, and therefore, by the time you offer your response, my thoughts will have carried me beyond the problem I first shared with you, you then will be able to appreciate that the solution you offer, although entirely appropriate for the original question, no longer addresses what is more important to me at the moment. I cannot, in good conscience, therefore, share with you the affirmation you deserve for the correct solution you have given me.

Thus, you will see that you cannot even depend on your creativity if, to feed it, you need the affirmation from a fickle and stingy world. What you need then, is to be able to secure another way of obtaining affirmation, another way of measuring yourself, so that you can be affirmed for what you truly are able to be rather than for being able to keep pace with an impossible situation.

You can measure yourself differently only if you truly are different from those things you can measure easily. If so, traditional methods will fail to identify you. If, using traditional methods, you succeed in being able to identify yourself fully, it shows only that you are not truly different. Then, you are doomed to tying to give account of yourself by satisfying a world that never can stay still long enough to be satisfied by your attempts to please it.

In order to be able to measure yourself and determine your identity, therefore, you must have at least a working knowledge of the things you can measure, why they can be measured, and by applying the same rules to yourself, whether you are governed by those parameters.

Only then will you be prepared to examine yourself without those diversions and determine an independent means of measuring who you are and what you can be. Only then will you be able to develop an objective that will be more appropriate to your relation to the world as it is rather than trying to adapt the world to be more appropriate to what you believe you should be.

Chapter 5.

Understanding Change and Determining its Limitations

If you look around in the room you occupy now, you will observe a number of situations which you may accept as the results of natural events. For example, you may turn on a radio and hear voices coming, apparently from nowhere. You know, however, that these sounds are created by the amplification of radio waves that are picked up by the radio antenna. In fact, you do not even think about what causes it, accepting the sound from the radio as a natural event. Similarly, because of the contributions of modern science, you have learned to accept that there are bacteria floating around the room, little squiggly monsters that can invade your body and cause you to become ill.

If instead, we were sitting in the same space five thousand years ago, and I were to make the same comment about those squiggly little monsters, or about those waves of energy that carry voices, you might not have stayed too close to me. You might have thought I was crazy, or worse, a consort of the devil. It is possible, also, that what I am about to discuss with you now may evoke the same fears.

What is important here, however, is that you understand that just as there were events which our ancestors did not understand and which they either dismissed as being unreal, or which they relegated to the supernatural, so too there are events which you do not understand now and, for similar reasons, still either relegate to the supernatural, or dismiss as figments of the imagination.

You may believe that you are much more sophisticated than they were, and that you have a better understanding of what is real. Yet, you too would have reacted just as they did, even to the things you understand now if you did not have the benefit of hindsight. What you know from the discoveries which gave you the hindsight, however, is but a miniscule portion of what still remains to be discovered. It is possible, therefore, that some of the things you presently dismiss as being unreal or perhaps as being some type of supernatural event can, at some time in the future, be seen to be as natural as you see those other things now.

We may have exhausted our understanding of the unknown as being squiggly little monsters. We may have demonstrated uses for most of the energy sources that could be harnessed. Yet, the unknown is still as fearful and as immense today as it was when it also contained things we now have the ability to identify and understand. What is more is that much of what we fear as the unknown is brought to us by the process of change in those things we already know and understand.

It is important, therefore, to see those events we accept as natural now from the perspective of our less enlightened ancestors in order, perhaps, to assess whether we are doing the same thing, albeit to a different set of events.

A metaphorical/historical observation of why the human being has been slow in addressing the issue of change.

Change has always been an enigma to the human being. Generally, we are so unsure of what we are or what we should be that we can feel secure only by fixing our individual identities to something stable. What we see of the world through the crude instruments that are easily available to us seems stable. So, we have learned to attach our identities to the world as we see it, unaware that those apparently stable objects are parts of a constantly moving universe.

Meanwhile, we know that the total universe is huge. It extends into a vast unknown, so vast that it always has been impossible for us to feel comfortable with the things with which we have chosen to identify because they seem to be puny and weak sections of the whole. The rest was always seen as the potential enemy, one that had such great authority over the small sections we can know, that we either must avoid it or obtain protection from it.

Therefore, to stay secure in such changing conditions we have learned to refuse to accept change as an integral part of those things we see as stable. If something happens to destabilize what we have learned to accept as stable, we either are oblivious to the change, or we view it as an abnormal disruption of a normal state caused by interference from some outside source. Then, it is easy to conclude that the change imposed on what we consider as being stable has been caused either by the inconsiderate activity of another person, or the manifestation of the power of an entity greater than ourselves.

As long as we are satisfied that the change is imposed by an entity over which we have no control, we have shown little desire to explore it further. Instead, we have, in the past, directed our efforts towards pacifying that more powerful entity and suppressing any exploration that might offend whomever or whatever that entity might be.

Take, for example, the way mankind viewed the universe, say five thousand years ago. The world was a flat surface on which we lived, and which had its boundaries beyond which we were not allowed. The rest of the universe was populated by more powerful entities who had dominance over us. Then, it was easy to explain any unnatural change as being the activity of one of these superhuman beings, or deities. Limited by the crudeness of the instruments available to us then, namely our five senses, it was easy to force ourselves to remain within the safety of what we could see and touch, and explain any changes to these as the activities of the deities.

Obviously, it would have been dangerous to explore any of those activities since such exploration would constitute insubordination, perhaps punishable by an act which would be more painful, and unleashed, perhaps, on a larger group of people. Therefore, it would have been necessary to establish a watchdog group who would function as liaisons between man and the deities, and who would ensure that nobody would do something that would bring down the wrath of the deities beyond that which already was displayed. Such a group were called the priests, and were even more powerful than the kings of any particular country.

Meanwhile, there always were events that were sufficiently far removed from our immediate environment and which we could have explored without such explorations being acts of insubordination. One of these was the movements of the stars. Our fears, however, prevented us from exploring that activity simply because they were seen as the movements of the chariots of the deities across the heavens, and therefore, sacred to those powerful beings.

Since any activity which changed our stable world could be explained as the activity of the deities, something which we could not dispute and had to accept, and since there was no need to explore the movement of the stars as that activity also was easily explained within the same definitions, there was nothing left to challenge our curiosity. Everything was explained. We became content to accept what was meted out to us, passively accepting our fate as toys for more powerful beings. We were kept in the dark by our basic ignorance which led to fears which fed that ignorance. I suppose that we would have remained in that ignorance had it not been for the visions of one man and the subsequent attempts of another to expand on that vision. But first, let us examine it in its proper sequence and see how the truth may have evolved.

How the stagnation was broken.

About five thousand years ago, in the very powerful city of Babylon, a poor goatherd named Abraham had a dream. In his dream, he was told that there was only one Deity. That Deity was all powerful and had authority over all men.

Just think of what might have been happening at that time. Abraham was no fool. He knew that Babylon was a powerful city with powerful governors. They believed that they achieved their status because they were favored by the deities, their deities. Abraham knew, therefore, that he could not reveal such a dream to the authorities of that place. He knew, however, that there were many people like himself, goatherds, who were forced to be nomads by the pressures of their trade. He could share his beliefs only with those people who happily welcomed the one deity concept.

Let us face it. As nomads, they were not considered part of the elite of that society, and thus, were not always welcome to participate in the sacrifices. They could do with a deity of their own. As nomads, it was difficult to carry around the requisite statues of the many deities. A Deity which was not only single but invisible, was easily transportable, a godsend so to speak, for a nomad.

A new explanation for the natural events in our environment was born. Theoretically, it should have allowed scientists to be free to question the activity of the stars, an activity which no longer could be explained as being the chariots of the deities. The new deity was single and invisible, and therefore, did not need chariots.

It must be remembered, however, that the people who carried this concept were seen as simple goatherds, not a group who wielded any authority or received any respect in the more sophisticated society. The ignorance persisted, therefore.

Those who had an interest in exploring the activity of the stars were prevented from doing so by their beliefs in the multi-deity concept. Those who were free to explore it because of their conviction in the one deity concept were too busy establishing their relationship to that private Deity that they did not have the time nor the inclination to explore the activity that would have given us our first explanation of the natural activity of change.

Despite this opportunity, we remained in ignorance for another three thousand years. One part of the world still worshipped many deities and prevented themselves from exploring a visible phenomenon. Another part of the world was free to explore a phenomenon which they could not see. What we needed was a way of connecting these two parts together. This was difficult because the fears of each side were so deep-set that anyone who tried to convince one of the other was immediately seen as a threat to the whole of society.

Then, about two thousand years ago, someone achieved it. Whether we see that person as a courageous and visionary man, a special messenger from the Deity, or the human manifestation of the Deity is irrelevant here. What happened could have been predictable. His deep conviction of the nature of the Deity and in the human connection to that Deity evoked the fears of both sides and had him killed, a consequence which he did not fear. This instilled a similar conviction in his followers, providing them with the courage to spread the word to the other section of society even though they knew that it would evoke the fears of these people and jeopardize their lives.

The ultimate effect on science of this merging of beliefs was not felt for many years, but the seed was sown. It was inevitable that those who wanted to explore the visibly unstable environment of the stars would be freed from the restrictions imposed by the fears that they were the personal chariots of the deities, and would proceed with such exploration.

The first recorded study was done in Alexandria, Egypt, in 150 A.D. by Ptolemy. He observed the movements of certain stars and designed what he referred to as the intergalactic clock. He referred all these movements to the earth as the central theme in this system. There was one major error in it because he also saw the sun as one of these planets revolving around the earth. The treatise was accepted by the established church as being in accordance with the teachings of Genesis in the bible, and therefore, not sacrilegious.

You must remember that this body represented the connection between the Deity and man, responsible for man's showing of respect to that Deity. They had the authority to condone or ban any act which could jeopardize the relationship between man and the Deity. The unexplained being explained as purposeful sources of light instead of randomly moving chariots, again as the activity of the Deity, the matter was laid to rest.

It was not until the year 1542 that an astronomer named Nicolaus Copernicus was able to query Ptolemy's theories successfully and suggest that the earth was a rapidly moving body, a movement which people do not sense because they too are moving with the earth at the same speed.

The church, however, could not accept this contradiction to the absolute power of the Deity as interpreted in the book of Genesis, and placed Copernicus' book on the prohibited list, preventing further exploration of the issue. Then, in 1632, at the University of Padua, now Italy, but then part of the Holy Roman Empire, another astronomer by the name of Galileo, with the advantage of a new instrument which extended the reach of the crude sense of vision, the telescope, was able to recognize the nature of some of the planets, and became further convinced of the accuracy of Copernicus' theories.

Galileo, however, was forced by the church to rescind his theories and abandon the Copernicus system. He was helped in this decision by the Inquisition which relieved him of his position and confined him to house arrest.

It was due to these acts of defiance by people who were willing to be condemned for their beliefs that the fears that we were not allowed to explore the universe by the selfishness of powerful Deities were laid to rest, and the search for a natural source of change was initiated.

The important point to observe from this dissertation is that our pervasive fears of the unknown have always prevented us from understanding what is there for us to understand. Whether we explain the unknown as the activity of a more powerful entity, or whether we simply ignore its presence, are we not also doing, on an individual basis, what we see now as the ignorant and frightened defensiveness of less enlightened people? Are we not also stifling our further understanding by hiding behind the protection of a different ignorance?

There are many examples of our subsequent search for the source of natural change. This search does not negate the presence of a powerful Deity. Instead, it recognizes that a better understanding of what can be measured, even with more sophisticated instruments, will provide a stronger basis for our acceptance of any less visible nature we may share with the less visible Deity.

The search for the source.

Following the pioneering work of these early scientists, there emerged a rapid proliferation of experiments and theories on the nature of our material environment and what causes it to change so readily. As new instruments were developed to extend our vision into what was immediately relevant, each layer, so to speak, was peeled back, revealing another problem that had to be solved.

In a simplified discourse, we can say that what instilled the fears in people were the activities of elements that were not obvious to them as being part of the natural environment. Therefore, when it first was discovered that apparently solid objects were not truly solid, but were composed of smaller parts called crystals, some of the activities were explained. The disintegration of what was seen as a stable entity could be explained as the release of the crystalline substructure of the object. Crystalline particles were too small to be seen with the naked eye. With the aid of magnifying instruments like the microscope, however, they were observed to exist freely, and therefore, with the capability of interfering with the crystals that form the solid object, thus changing the appearance of that object.

One source of change was revealed. It did not explain all change. It however, exonerated the Deity from being directly involved in the change. It also proved that the change was not a purposeful imposition by some greater entity intended as a punitive measure towards the human race.

Since the human body was an object whose solidity was similar to this, it too must be composed of a sub-structure of a crystalline nature. These crystalline structures were seen as cells. Cells could exist freely as well as being joined together to form an apparently solid object. Those free cells are not visible to the naked eye. Therefore, they could move about undetected, and interfere with the cells that form the body.

Freely mobile cells are called bacteria. Bacterial cells are only cells, similar to the body's cells, but cells that have adapted to an environment different from that of the body. Their presence in the body only serves to let them compete with the body's cells for survival. Disease then, was no longer seen as the wrath of the Deity. We were beginning to see it as the normal activity of a highly mobile object, the body, integrating with similar activity in an extensive universe. When something happens to throw it off its balance, we now see that as something which could be reversed or even prevented, simply by restoring the previous balance.

This discovery, however, did not explain much of what was happening. Surely, the disintegration of apparently solid objects was not confined to their breakdown into their crystalline sub-structure. Surely, also, the presence of other types of activity could not be explained by the free movement of crystals.

This search for further explanation into the cause of less detectable activity without going the easy route of ascribing it to an act of the Deity, led to the discovery of molecules as smaller building blocks which comprised the larger building blocks. With the discovery of molecules, another series of events was explained. The free movement of an even less visible entity could explain some of the activities that caused change. The freer these sub-structures were seen to be, the more obvious it became that the effects of their activities were the result of random movement. In short, much of the changes were not purposeful acts, but were the results of an activity that permeated every object.

Each time a new sub-structure was discovered, it explained another activity. It also showed that the apparent disintegration of what we saw as solid objects was not the destruction of the material at all. In fact, it was the release of the object into the smaller particles that formed it.

Each succeeding particle was observed to be formed by the integration of a group of even smaller particles, and therefore, revealed activities that were less visible to the naked eye, or to the instruments that were designed to view the previous particle.

What became more intriguing, however, was that each time we were able to identify a new sub-structure, it was observed to be more mobile than the larger particle it formed. Therefore, it explained why so much activity was happening to the objects we thought to be stable. It did not explain what causes each smaller particle to be so active, however.

One thing it showed was that the events that occurred in the world became less likely to be a direct interference by a Deity . The search became more intense for the reasons that such activity occurs. Many complex theories have been put forward, each respecting the possible effect of such a powerful entity as a Deity, but each focussed on the activities as being self sustained, even if initiated by such a source.

The unfolding of the secrets of the activities of the forces that affect the structures we can identify continued in what I consider the onion skin effect. Many prominent scientists contributed in that unveiling process. With the discovery of the atom, even more explanations became available. When Lord Rutherford was able to split the atom in 1895, until then thought to be the smallest particle to form the visible of the universe, the explanation for yet another activity was available. Lightening, for example, could be explained as the activity of free electrons. These were considered to be negatively charged particles that, joined with similar particles, formed the atom, and so on to the more solid structures we observe in our environment. Activities that were thought to be distinct from matter were discovered to be part of the whole range of particles that formed matter.

Then, newer, more sophisticated instruments were developed. The electron, proton, and neutron, particles which could only be differentiated by their behaviours towards each other, were discovered to be formed of smaller particles which were even freer and thus more active than the electrons. At this point, the term 'quark' was used to designate those smaller particles.

These smaller particles were so active that their activity within any object could be the source of much change within that object, other change being induced by their activity outside that object, affecting it. In order to possess such constant activity, however, it is necessary that these particles have some inherent property whose main effect is to generate activity. If not, we are back to the same stage as we were five thousand years ago, explaining all change as the imposition of the supernatural on a submissive world, albeit through a more indirect approach.

The rules governing the activity of the source.

Then, in 1905, Albert Einstein, after observing a simple activity while working as a clerk in the Swiss patent office, suggested that if, as with all other things, light was also a particle, in this case a photon, the light he observed coming from the clock would have reached his eyes a fraction of a second after it left the clock. Then, what he saw as three o'clock, for instance, was seen a fraction of a second after three. He went on to suggest that if he were to climb onto that particle of light leaving the clock at a particular time, he would always see that time, even many hours later.

This seems to be an obvious statement now. You must realize, however, that it is true only if light behaves like a particle, albeit extremely small. These were followed by more serious observations which suggested that quantum particles, those miniscule particles that are the basis of every material object, behaved like particles that were affected by the presence of other similar particles.

In fact, the general law of relativity suggests that every particle existing in space is affected by the presence of every other particle. This, certainly, is based on these particles having the same property that induces activity. What seemed to be the reason for their behaviour was that each particle possessed a sort of energy charge, perhaps electromagnetic, perhaps some other similar energy.

If that is the case, we then will discover that these particles move in what has been described as a wave, presumably because they respond to the forces from all the other similar particles in all directions. Because the freely moving particles are so small compared to the range of sizes which the composites of other particles in space can have, the forces acting on each of them will be varied and numerous, coming from so many directions, including other freely moving particles.

Then, the movements of these free particles can never be straight, but will follow a more curved path, the tightness of the curve (or frequency of each wave) probably being influenced by the distribution of the other particles around it. They then will induce different effects on the instruments which you use to measure them. Particles moving at one frequency will, for example, stimulate the rods and cones of the eye, and will be termed light. Particles moving at a different frequency will stimulate a photographic plate, and may be described as X-rays, and so on.

In fact, this is the process by which you measure any object. Particles leaving that object affect the instrument you use to measure it. The instrument, in turn, undergoes a change which you observe, allowing you to draw the conclusion that such an object is present.

Perhaps, you will be able to visualize it better if you see it in terms of what you consider reality. When you touch something, what happens is that the forces from that object irritates some cells that are located in your skin. These cells, by being irritated, undergo a temporary change causing them to initiate an electrochemical response. This is taken by the nerves to the brain, letting you know that there is an object present, and also how hard it is. The fact that there are many cells over a small area also allows you to have a comparative idea of the surface, and so determine whether it is rough or smooth.

Similarly, you see because light photons reflect off an object and stimulate the rods and cones in your retina. If these particles did not leave the object, you will not see it. What you see is the light from the object. You identify the object by the comparative amounts of light reflected from surrounding objects.

You see a particular color because all of the range of vibrating particles do not reach your eyes all the time. Sometimes a certain range of light activity comes, stimulating a section of rods and cones at one stage, another set by a different range, giving you a comparative view of the world which you interpret as color. It is said that objects have no color, however. They have properties which absorb certain parts of the light spectrum, allowing you to see the parts that are reflected.

The point is that you measure things because they emit particles that affect the instruments you use to measure them. The more precise the instruments are, the smaller the emission you are able to measure.

Prior to this discovery of the general law of relativity, another theory was put forward. This was called the specific theory of relativity. It recognizes a simple error in our ability to measure anything. This is the fact that if the instruments are stimulated by the objects because their particles affect the particles that comprise the instruments, so too the particles from the instruments must have an effect on the object they are measuring. This is comparable to trying to report on how a child plays by himself while being in the room with the child. What he does, knowing that you are present, is different from what he does if he truly is alone. Therefore, what you see is different from what really is there.

Some Practical Conclusions.

You now can draw a series of conclusions from this information so that it is more applicable to a less abstract view of the world. The first conclusion you can form is that if something exists as matter, it either exists as a quark particle or some composite of quark particles, being atoms, molecules, or larger, more distinct objects. Then it will have a property which allows it to be measured by the way its composite particles affect another object, namely the instrument.

The second conclusion you can form is that, because that which you can measure is either a single, highly energized particle or a composite of such particles, what you identify cannot stay that way. It either will be broken down into its composite parts if it is a composite, or will be drawn to other similar particles and form a composite. In other words, by being able to measure something, you will have determined that such an existent is unstable. It will either be 'destroyed' by being separated into its composite, or distorted by being drawn into another composite.

The third conclusion you can form is that if you can measure something, it follows that it is composed of such particles that affect other similar particles, and therefore, will fall under the general rule governing such entities. That is, what you measure cannot be the same by the time you have finished measuring it. It exists in a state of constant change.

The last conclusion you can form is that if you cannot measure something which you believe to exist, it either does not truly exist or exists as an energy source with different energy from that which has been determined to be possessed by matter, be it electromagnetic, quantum energy, or whatever term you choose to describe it. If you know it exists, then it just is not matter.

The behaviours of entities that are governed by that source.

Why are we discussing this difficult subject? We are doing so in order to show that you cannot do anything about the activities that are happening to the world which we can measure. Nature exists because of this activity. As a result, the world, by its very nature, is destined to be in a constant state of change.

What you see as matter is only a stage in a continuous transition of those particles. They move so constantly that they always will form some object which, relative to another object, can be determined to have some size, shape, color, or texture. That object, however, lasts only as long as the particles forming it stays within the same relation to each other and to the rest of particles outside of it.

The movement is so continuous that the object is never that object for more than a miniscule amount of time. But, because our instruments are crude, we do not observe the transition until it has progressed beyond a significant stage. It is probably because the instruments are also going through the same transition that we can continue to measure the object as being stable, relative to the instrument.

It reminds me of a television show where the woman says to her spouse that she was unhappy that she was getting older and less attractive. Her spouse responded that his eyes too were getting old and weak at the same pace. Therefore, she still looked as attractive to him as the day they met.

You can visualize this by thinking of yourself as being large enough to view the universe as a whole, from the outside. What you will see is a veritable cauldron of activity. Within the composite of that which is limited to what you know of as matter, there is constant activity. As one section seems to be destroyed, the composite parts separate and move to other sections, distorting what was there and forming what seems to be a new creation, only to continue moving so that the new creation is destroyed as easily as it was formed.

Even more down-to-earth, is the observation of a group of people performing at a stadium during intermission. They each have a specific path to follow, constantly moving. Yet, as viewed from above, what you see is the formation of, now a flag, now a flower, now a message. Just remember that, in terms of the universe, the individuals are so miniscule and numerous, and the product so vast, that the obvious transition of this observable product occurs over longer time frames.

The time, from the destruction of one section and the temporary formation of another as the individual particles continue to move, are measured in light years. Thus, it is easy to see why you can be led into the belief that, in the miniscule time frame of a few years, everything seems stable. In a fair comparison, you must view the movements at the stadium in time frames of fractions of a second. Then, those pictures, either of the flag or of the message will appear to be stable and permanent.

Reality versus symbolism.

A conclusion you also can draw from this is that matter is not reality. Reality is the particle, or perhaps energy source, that gives rise to the forces that allow the particles to form what we can observe as matter. The object we observe is only that object as long as the tiny sub atomic particles continue to interrelate in the same way they did to form the object. As soon as they are arranged differently, the object disappears.

To illustrate this, think of a fist. A fist is a fist as long as you close your fingers tightly together. The fingers are real. The fist is a perception. It exists only because the fingers are together. If you separate your fingers, the fist no longer exists. What you have is an open palm. Similarly, your body is your body as long as those proteins, minerals and carbohydrates are in the relation they need to be in order to form what you recognize as your body. There will come a time when those same building blocks will be reorganized to form daisies, for example.

What exists, then, is interrelationship. The object you can identify exists only while the particles that form it continue to be in the same interrelationship as they were when they first were joined together to form that object. If you can restructure those particles, the original object will cease to exist. Something else will exist in its place.

Matter, then, is not reality. Rather, the energy source which allows the formation of matter, is reality. The thing which you cannot measure, the quantum particle, is more real than the thing you can measure, the object. When you can measure something, therefore, you are measuring only the aggregation of the base energy, the transitional stage in the activity of a reality.

Look around you. According to this logic, the chair you are sitting in is not real. It feels real because you are perceiving it through an instrument, your body, which responds to the same forces that are aggregated to form the chair. There are so many 'kazillions' of those particles that, even though many of them have proceeded onwards, no longer part of the chair, the transitional structure of the chair will appear to remain intact for some time. This may seem to be such a long time of transition that you possibly can accept it as stable. Just remember, however, that what to you is a long time is only a miniscule stage in the transition of those particles.

In addition, you can destroy that chair by burning it. What you will have accomplished is a destruction only of the way the particles interrelated to form the chair.

The freed particles can restructure themselves to form something else somewhere else. They cannot be destroyed. They may not be accessible to the instruments with which you can measure them, but they still exist, even freely dispersed in a wider area of the universe.

It can be assumed that measurement is possible only because some sensory input in your body has been stimulated by some activity which we now know to indicate energy in transition . Regardless of how sophisticated your instruments may be, they only magnify the instruments with which you were born. Therefore, any instrument which you can operate using any of your five senses is an instrument which can measure only the activity of matter as an activity of quantum particles. When you become aware of something, that thing must, therefore, be matter because you are aware of it, directly or indirectly, through your five senses.

Matter, then, is something which can be measured. It exists only as an interrelation of what is real. Matter can be destroyed. The interrelationship is destroyed, not the reality which forms that relationship. Matter can be created, simply by restructuring the interrelationship of the energy particles of which all matter is formed.

If an energy source exists but can neither be measured nor restructured, it also cannot be destroyed. It is not made up of interrelating parts. It is not matter. It must have properties that are different from the property which makes quantum particles attract each other, whether this is the electromagnetic property, or some other undefined energy force.

A hypothesis on the nature of that which cannot be measured.

Many theories have been put forward to explain the extent of the universe. Many of these theories are offered while considering only what we know as space using what we know as instruments. They do not always consider that space can also be what does not contain matter. If you will think about the enormity of the galaxy, and beyond that, the other galaxies we can observe, and try to extrapolate that to the possible extent of the universe, you will become so lost that you will be confused.

You also will recognize how insignificant are the things we fight over in our little section of the world, and how insignificant you are as a measurable entity. The discovery almost begs that you not be such a measurable entity. Yet, how can you know whether there is such an energy source that is not confined by the properties of matter? The fact is that you cannot know that for sure. What you can study, however, are whether an energy source which is not matter can exist, what possible properties such an energy source can have, and how such a source of energy can relate to the material universe without being matter.

Yet, if you will consider the properties which govern what we can measure and identify, you will realize that particles endowed with that type of energy must be contained within their own self imposed space. Within that space which must be large enough to contain all the numerous particles so energized, there will be enormous forces created by greater aggregates of these particles, concentrated within some central core.

This will create its own self imposed boundary. Nothing can be measured beyond that boundary since nothing that can measure the properties of matter can be taken outside that boundary. We must realize that we cannot be so conceited to presume that just because we can measure one type of energy force, no other type exists. If any other type exists, such an energy force will not be defined within the limitations of matter. Such an energy force, then, will not have size as this is a property that is relative to the instrument which is measuring it. It cannot have color as color is only the ability of an object to reflect light, an energy force related to matter. It cannot have shape nor location as these are properties that are relative to the parts that form the object, or parts that are adjacent to it.

If such an energy force exists, it will be powerful and indestructible. Something is destructible when it is a composite of smaller sub-parts in the first place. An energy force which does not have the attractive/repulsive properties of matter cannot be so composed, and is thus a self contained entity. It is immune to the instabilities inherent in matter. It cannot, therefore, be destroyed, distorted, or created. Such an energy source also does not have to have any direct input in the activity of matter for matter to be any more unstable than it already is.

It also is possible that many such energy forces can exist, perhaps as independent forces with the same nature, or perhaps as different forces, extending through a whole range of possibilities. If such energy forces do exist, they will co-exist without interfering with each other as material forces do since their properties do not include those attractive/repulsive forces that are common to matter.

Epilogue.

As a human being, you have learned to define your identity by attaching it to something stable. You now see that everything you can identify is so unstable that what you have learned to measure of them is determined by their instabilities. You may not always recognize the instabilities immediately. You know, however, that people frequently are surprised when they are rejected by, separated from, or have inaccessibility to those things they believe to be able to give them stability.

You can see that such unpreparedness is unwarranted. The fears of losing what they are destined to lose; the discomfort of being left naked when the inevitable separation occurs; the stress of trying to reach something that will always be inaccessible; all these experiences are unnecessary if you only will recognize how unstable what we see as stable can be.

Then, you will have only two choices in deciding how you relate to such a changing environment. The first is to approach it with fatalism. The second is to approach it with detachment.

Fatalism suggests that if you are going to be destroyed by the unstable environment in any case, you should enjoy what you can enjoy for as long as it is available to you. You also will be prepared, like the grunion quoted in the second chapter, to fit in with the environment, existing as long as the environment lets you exist, experiencing as much comfort as the environment lets you experience.

Detachment suggests that you examine yourself to see how you may be different from the energy type that responds to the laws governing the behaviour of matter. You may discover that you do not need to attach yourself to anything in order to achieve some stability. You may be able to stand alone. You also may discover that, in order to be able to stand alone, you may have to do something more than passive existence allows you to do. If such is the case, you, at least, will have an objective, and the information you need for making your choice, fatalism or detachment.

Chapter 6.

Developing a Secure Identity.

Once, I was speaking to a colleague about the young daughter of a mutual friend. This girl had recently run away from home, stating that she needed to find herself. My friend commented that he could not understand the impetuousness of youth. He suggested that this girl's father should take her to the nearest mirror and show her herself. She then would be free to address more important pursuits.

Regardless of how chagrined you may feel by such a show of autocracy, it is important to use it to discover whether you feel the same way about who or what the human being is, and if not, whether you have an acceptable alternative for your definition of the person. Many people do what we have seen our ancestors do, and accept the presence of something by relegating it to some area of the world which they do not understand. By association, this undefined existent is accepted as being part of that complex area. For example, you accept that you think with your brain. Yet, you do not usually question how this happens. The act of thinking is boxed in with the unknown function of the brain.

You, as any other human being, do not always want to accept that you are just what you observe as a deteriorating body supporting a mind which, magically, does not deteriorate with the body. You want, in fact, to be an existent which can function through that sophisticated body, even if you also must be attached to it.

You, as any other human being, do not always want to be some unknown physical existent, wandering through this life with no measurable objective, yet being required to fulfil an obligation to some intangible part of yourself which you are not even sure exists.

If, therefore, the purpose of this work is to help you discover an identity which is immune to the effects of a world that, by its own structure, cannot be stable, you must have a definition of who or what you are, one that is more tangible than the definition you can get from blind faith or a reflective mirror. The search for the person makes sense only if you can accept that the person cannot be what you can see and measure within the body. That does not necessarily have to be a religious experience even though religion is dedicated to the recognition of an existent which is beyond the measurable universe.

Religion does not have to be right. We may discover that the person can exist without having to be subservient to an existent which is greater than the measurable universe. Religion, however, is not necessarily wrong. If we discover that such an entity greater than the measurable universe exists, we will have to admit that such an entity has all right to our respect and subservience.

This treatise, however, is intended to deal with you as an entity. If you, as that entity, can be seen to be detached from the things that define the measurable universe, you will be able to function independent of the things that are known to be unstable. You are free to interpret how you assess yourself then, maybe as a stable entity, maybe as one with a different type of instability. If you wish, you can accept and respect the existence of something greater than you and as much a detached entity as you are.   If you wish, you still may pursue an independent goal as that entity if you interpret that there is no greater power beyond your own existence which you must accept or respect.

Regardless of how you define the person, you must concede that mankind has always been intrigued by the presence of feelings, understanding, and reason as properties which human beings possess, and which makes us into the unique entities that we consider ourselves to be. The continuous frustration, however, is that it has always been difficult to locate these properties. You may think, and, if you can clear your mind of presumptions, you will find that it is difficult to locate where in the recognizable body this function takes place.

Feelings, however, seem to be more localized. Despite this, no one has ever been able to locate feelings either. This may not be because they are not measurable. We now have greater insight into some of those things that have always been inaccessible to our less sophisticated instruments. We know now that such inaccessibility does not necessarily indicate that the entity is unmeasurable; we know that it may have been the result of an activity that was inaccessible only to our available instruments.

It is possible, therefore, that with the advantage of hindsight, we can observe how we have evolved into our present presumptions about the location of the human psyche, and perhaps, determine whether such presumption is accurate.

Search for the Intellect.

The assumption which is most common in our modern world is that the brain, as the central coordinator of the whole body, also is host to the mind. Thought, it is considered, occurs through specific functions of the brain. The source of these functions has never been isolated, however.

This assumption has not always been accepted. One of the more widely accepted philosophy was that published by Rene Descartes in 1642 A.D. This held that the human being was a dual entity, consisting of a material body controlled by an immaterial mind. This philosophy so influenced people's acceptance of the nature of the human person as an immaterial entity that behavioural disorders were, for a long, time considered to be the result of that person being possessed by the devil.

It was not until the emergence of Sigmund Freud who saw abnormal behaviour as the result of both environmental and genetic factors that many people escaped the rigors of repeated exorcism, or rejection by society as evil forces. This may not have been the intent of Descartes, but it was the interpretation which survived at the time. In our more enlightened era, we have accepted that a person's behaviour emanates from the brain, and subsequently, originates there.

So great is the fear that any other interpretation will again leave us vulnerable to the possibility that a person's behaviour is controlled by an inaccessible force such as an immaterial mind, that we are afraid to question the validity of the conclusion that the brain is the source, not just of the stimulations that activate the body, but of thought itself.

We already have grown past some of the other possibilities like the heart when we decided on the brain as the central core of the person. That may have been a wise move since recent trends in surgical procedures have included complete heart transplants, proving that the person neither dies with the heart, nor is exchanged for the person whose heart subsequently occupies the body. There also is no other area of the body which can be suggested to house the functions of the mind since, with modern surgical techniques, people have been observed to have many of these areas removed while still retaining total mental functions.

You do know, however, that it is impossible for us to gain access to you if your brain is removed. This, obviously, is a possibility if you, the person, are the brain or some vital part of it. It also can happen if the brain is only the medium through which you can stimulate the body to reveal yourself to us. If it is the latter, its removal only prevents you from revealing yourself, it does not mean that you are no longer alive any more than being asleep means that you are dead. If then, the person is generated by the brain or any part of it, it must be shown that the person, as determined by the presence of reason, understanding, and emotion, will die if that part dies, and will be accessible if that part remains intact.

Locating the Intellect.

There is one thing of which you can be sure in our present era, is that we have the capacity to measure anything which can be measured, or at least, some activity which indicates its presence. You no longer have to rely on what once was thought to be the absolute indication of the existence of something, its tangible presence. You know that even an electron is an existent. The fact that it moves so rapidly that it can only be measured by its activity does not preclude its presence, even if that is so for a miniscule amount of time.

Therefore, you have the capacity to locate the person. All you need are the readings of those instruments which measure each level of presence or activity. If the mind is a physical entity, rather than presuming its nature, you will be able to determine it. If the mind is not a physical entity, you will fail in that attempt regardless of how precise your instruments are.

With that as a hypothesis, you can start with a crude examination of the brain, and proceed through more and more sophisticated measurements until you find an entity or a function which, if stimulated, will cause your reason, understanding, or emotions, to become more intense, and if reduced, will cause the opposite effect. You also must be willing to make logical deductions from those findings.

The first logical deduction that is necessary is to conclude that if the mind is the result of the function of the whole brain, you will lose part of those three mental functions if even a part of the brain has been damaged. Without any special instruments, you know that this is not so. People have been known to have full mental function after having surgery removing part of their brain.

You also can know that there is no separate segment of the brain which is devoted to the functions of thinking, understanding, or reason. Neuroanatomists have dissected the brain and discovered that it is divided into distinct lobes. Each lobe has been followed through its nerve fibers to the spinal cord and found to be specific for some function of the body. For, example, there is the speech center, vision area, motor area, and so on.

Do not be fooled by the differentiation of the brain cells into the cortex and medulla. That differentiation only recognizes that one, the cortex, is the aggregate of neurons or brain cells, while the other, the medulla, is an aggregate of nerve fibers connecting different parts of the brain to each other and to the rest of the body. Therefore, when I refer to the brain being divided into lobes, I am referring to the cerebral cortex.

The only part of the brain which is not so connected with a specific function of the body are the frontal lobes. The fibers from these lobes, instead of being connected with the body, seemed to supply only the other parts of the brain. This led researchers to suggest that they were the brain to the rest of the brain as much as the rest of the brain was the brain to the body.

Many years and many frontal lobotomies later, this idea was rejected. The true function of the frontal lobes still is not known. What is known, however, is that their removal does not allow the reversal of behavioural abnormalities. What also is known is that, after a total lobotomy, a person still has the understanding he had before surgery, still could reason on new problems, and still could respond with appropriate emotions. In other words, the removal of the frontal lobes does not remove the mental function of the person.

The lobes of the brain, however, are made up of special cells called neurons, the source of a person's outward expression. A neuron can initiate activity from the brain. It, however, cannot initiate thought. A simple experiment will illustrate this.

Listen carefully to the sounds around you! You will hear sounds that you were not hearing a short time ago while you were engrossed in reading this material. Now you can return to focussing your attention on reading, and again, you can gradually dismiss those sounds. The point is that you can dismiss them even though they are there. Between the origin of the sound and your perception of them, it is not possible for such qualification.

Sound, as a vibration of the molecules of the medium through which it passes, air in this case, continues to exist as long as the vibrations exist. Your ear, passive receptors of this vibration, cannot but respond to it and transmit that vibration through some small bones to the cochlea. Here, a fluid takes up the vibration, transmitting it to some tiny fibers hanging in it, and causing some cells to be sufficiently irritated to start an electrical current in the hearing nerve.

This happens whenever there is sound reaching your ear. Your brain cells cannot but be stimulated by the activity of the nerve bringing the perception to it. This, by the way, is a similar process for any sense, from touch to vision. Since these nerve impulses cannot but respond to all of the sounds reaching them, it follows that your brain cells, those associated with hearing, cannot but be stimulated by all the sounds reaching your ears. If your mental function was a result of the activation of those cells, you cannot but be made aware of, either all the sounds reaching your ear, or by default, the most prominent ones.

This, as you know, is not the case. You can divert your attention to the most interesting sound or the most threatening one, even if that sound was the softest one reaching your ear. You can turn off your attention while someone is speaking to you, even though that person's voice still activates the cells of the hearing center of your brain. What is more is that such information is not stored unconsciously for you to retrieve when you are ready to pay attention to it. Conscious activity, therefore, must occur beyond the level of the cells of the brain. As we have discovered, the next logical level should be the molecular level, that of the chemicals of the brain.

The brain cells produce many chemicals that are unique to the brain. Some of these chemicals have been isolated. Others still remain elusive. If your mental activities, including feelings, are the result of the activity of such chemicals as is a popular perception in some circles, it is logical to presume that the manipulation of those chemicals can affect your mental function.

It also will be logical to presume that any condition which reduces the concentration of those chemicals also will reduce your mental function. As we mentioned earlier, many of these chemicals have not been isolated. The frustrations which medical science experiences in trying to manipulate these chemicals and so treat emotional disturbances does not prove that mental function is not related to chemicals. It proves only that it is not related to those chemicals which have been isolated and used. Those that appear to work also do not prove that mental function is a result of those chemicals. They simply can be shown to affect the medium through which information can be transmitted to your brain cells or from those cells.

Then, in the late seventies, a startling discovery made this even more relevant. Three people were found to have hydrocephalus while still functioning normally, two as college students and one as a factory worker. (Hydorcephalus is a condition which exists when the overflow drainage of excess fluids from the brain through a natural opening to the spinal cord has been blocked. In babies, this causes the head to swell to large proportions. In adults whose skulls are more rigid, no changes are obvious on the outside, but the accumulation of fluid on the inside causes the brain to be pushed aside until it becomes paper-tissue thin.)

In these people, their brains were discovered, because of routine CAT scans, to be paper-tissue thin. Special investigations relating the activities of the brain to corresponding activities of the body showed those associations to have remained intact.

Regardless of the type of chemicals that might have been produced by the brain, such chemicals would either have been accumulated in excessively large quantities over the years, or produced in extremely reduced quantities as a result of the compression. What was noticed because of the routine reasons for the scan, was that these people led normal lives, neither being overly intelligent nor completely stupid.

There are no special elements common to the brain that may suggest mentation at the atomic level. The brain, however, as with any other nervous tissue, carries electrical impulses. If the electrical activity within the brain is the process of thinking, a hypothesis upheld in some circles, you will expect that the manipulation of that electrical activity will affect emotional states, thinking, or understanding. You also will expect that any reduction or diversion of such activity will reduce those three functions.

It has been observed that if there is interference with the electrical activity of your brain, as happens in shock therapy or stroke, your capacity to express yourself coherently is reduced. After the acute situation has passed, however, you will regain the full ability to reason, emote, and understand. The loss of expression during the acute stage can easily be explained as damage to your capacity to express your thoughts, not necessarily formulate them. The return to full function after such injury suggests that thought could not be the result of electrical activity since the chronic effects of such an injury, such as a stroke, will continue to reduce or divert normal electrical activity and so will definitely reduce your your capacity to think.

This leaves us with the smallest particle known to man, the quantum particle. You know that we have the ability to measure quantum activity. If conscious thought results from the quantum activity of the brain, you should discover that its activity will fluctuate with fluctuations of emotions, thinking, or insight. If such an association cannot be demonstrated, it would mean that the mind is neither quantum activity nor any function which can affect quantum activity.

To conduct this experiment, you will require an EEG (electroencephalograph), and some volunteers. You will ask each volunteer to experience various fluctuations in mental activity, like concentration on solving a mathematical problem, reacting to sad news, day dreaming, or sleeping. If you were to do this experiment, you would discover as some researchers did, that the EEG readings remain constant even though the mental activities of the volunteers are changing.

All that you will be able to conclude from the process of logic is that you cannot measure the existence of the person by measuring the physical extremes of the body. The person, the conscious activity with which you and everyone else identifies, can only be said to exist as an entity which is not measurable as matter.

The Reality of Conscious Energy.

From the information discussed in the previous chapter, you will know that the discovery that the human mind does not have properties associated with matter does not necessarily relegate the mind to being some ethereal substance, but suggests that, as an entity, it must exist outside of the limitations of matter.

This means that, as a mind, you must be an energy source which is not matter. This argument is not intended only to determine what the mind is, from an observation of what it is not. We know that it cannot be a composite of smaller units as this will require that there be some form of attraction/repulsion effect of smaller units on each other, a property that will allow it to be measured.

With regards to matter, the true entity must be the quark particle, or the quantum energy which activates it, not any of the composite forms. Matter can only be destroyed or distorted to the level of this basic entity. Such an entity, by no longer being a composite of smaller parts cannot, therefore, be destroyed. Only the relationship between adjacent entities can be destroyed or distorted.

With regards to the human being, the true entity may be described as conscious energy. It is a basic entity, one which, by not being the interrelation between smaller sub-parts, is a complete entity. It, therefore, like the basic entity of matter, also cannot be destroyed. For the same reasons, it cannot be assumed that conscious energy can be distorted by some other conscious energy to form a different entity now, or in some future existence.

As such an entity, the mind, person, soul, consciousness, or whatever name you give it, cannot have color as color is the behaviour of light particles reflected from an object, an event which requires the attractive/repulsive forces associated with matter. Consciousness also cannot have size or shape because size or shape is a measure of existence relative to the location of other units or a composite of such units.

Another significant advantage for the human mind to be such an immaterial entity is that you can expand your mind, and even if you use the insight of another person to acquire the information necessary to do so, that other person will not be depleted of what he or she may have shared. In fact, the other person can also grow by the act of sharing. A material object, on the other hand, can be enlarged, but to do so, you must deplete some other area of the material you have used.

An Uncomplicated Objective.

Now that we have succeeded in questioning whatever beliefs you may have had about your identity, it is time for you to take a look, instead, at yourself as conscious energy and understand what it means to be such. One thing you do know is that, as such an existent, your basic need, one that is common to anything that exists, is the need to be respected as what you are, sufficient to be allowed to be that entity without prejudice or provocation.

As conscious energy, this is possible only because, as a true entity which is not a transitional composite of smaller particles, its existence is stable. You do not have to be any more than you are just to continue to exist as conscious energy. What has to be obtained, however, is the experience of being significant as such an existent. You know that you are significant as an existent when you can contribute of yourself, something that is yours, created by you, or earned by you. When you reach that stage, you enjoy the contentment that what you are is as good as or better that what you were designed to be. You are fulfilled.

If as conscious energy, the product of your activity is insight, you become more significant the more insight you can create. If the rate of creation of such insight is dependent on the momentum of conscious energy, you become more significant the greater your momentum as a conscious energy. The more you use that energy to create insight, the more insight there is to allow you greater significance. Then the more fulfilled you will be. Your objective, then, has to be to develop a momentum of creativity, one that will allow you as much insight as you can need at any time. How can you determine if this is true, that your significance can be tied to your ability to create insight ? You can determine this simply by examining yourself and observing what you are now that allows you to be of any greater significance than you were when you were born.

Concentrate on yourself for a moment. Check the improvements you have made since you were born. You may start from any objective. You may examine many areas which you believe have been improved. Yet, if you examine them closely, you will observe that any apparent improvement is relative to some arbitrary value.

Material wealth is so relative to the desire of others to obtain it that it cannot be considered a dependable asset. (Owning a large acreage in Antarctica is not a dependable asset, for example). Your body may have become stronger in muscular size. But it is a gain over which you have so little control that a miniscule organism can destroy it. Its strength cannot be considered to be a dependable an asset since illness can destroy that strength regardless of your most valiant efforts. What is more, is that the cells are less supple than they were as a baby. They are reduced in vigor.

There is only one asset in which you have had any true improvement, and that is your insight. You have a greater understanding of the world and of yourself today than you were when you were born, or even yesterday. You also know that all of that insight was developed by the activity of your conscious energy, your creativity. You created the insight. The greater the momentum of that creativity, the greater the development of your insight. It stands to reason, therefore, that, to develop yourself to your greatest potential, you need to stimulate your creativity, the more effort you direct as it, the more efficient its development will be.

When you think of it, however, it seems so strange that people spend so much time trying to reach many other less stable objectives which neither add to their identity nor make it more secure, while the only gain they ever make is that of the development of their conscious energy. It seems strange that they would expend so much effort presuming that the gains they make are true gains when those objectives actually change independent of their efforts, sometimes in direction they choose, sometimes in the opposite direction. Then, their gains must really be only passive gains, their losses passive losses.

There are many people who have devoted their energies to securing physical survival by rigidly balancing their diets and avoiding all responsibility that leads to stress, still having to face an untimely death, either from the very problems they were trying to avoid, or from some unassociated condition. You must be careful not to conclude, just because you have done what you understand to be correct and have survived, that your success is the result of your focus on surviving any more than you can blame failures on your inability to take all possible precautions.

There once was a story told of a man who stood at a corner in Times Square in New York, clapping every fifteen minutes on the quarter hour. When an observer questioned the strangeness of his actions, he explained that he was doing it to keep away the elephants. The observer assured him that there were no elephants in New York city. The man, however, interpreted this as meaning that his plan was working.

Another man, at a different corner, may be stamping his feet at similar intervals for the same reason. Neither will want to stop and consider the other's solution because each one believes that it is his action which brings on the desired objective, and cannot, therefore, cannot be discontinued.

It is easy to see the stupidity in such an action. Yet, you do it daily. I do it daily. In fact it is the action of everyone in this world. We spend our time trying to survive, a feat over which we have no control. While we are surviving, we believe that it is due to our specific efforts. That is why every single person believes that he or she has the correct approach to life, simply because he (she) is surviving.

That is why, despite the fact that your only gain has been conscious development, you still are inclined to devote your time towards securing survival, a feat over which you have no control. It is time, therefore, for you to do the sensible thing, and give more attention to acquiring what you can acquire and less on the wasted effort of securing what you cannot secure, regardless of what you do. If, as that reality, conscious energy, the only achievement you have made or can make is to grow, is it not obvious that your objective is just that, to grow?

You start life as a miniscule conscious energy with the potential to grow. You have the opportunity to grow into someone who can contribute the unique contents of your conscious energy. Is it not obvious, then, that your objective, in attempting to grow is to develop momentum in that conscious energy as efficiently as you can? You cannot be efficient if, by focussing on what you cannot achieve, you attain only the minimum gains on what you do achieve, simply as the fallout from those other endeavors.

c

You are born as a
force of conscious
awareness with
only the potential
for creativity

Your creativity
grows as you use
it. You attain a
momentum of
growth which is
unique too you.

Figure 4. YOUR DEVELOPMENT AS CONSCIOUS ENERGY

Therefore, you will recognize that any greater use of creativity will lead to a corresponding growth in insight, and as a result, the opportunity for a similar growth in fulfilment, depending on the efficiency with which you measure yourself. Then, you will have accomplished that which you have the ability to accomplish, a greater momentum of conscious energy.

A look at an ultimate objective.

You will see, then, that there is a good incentive to know yourself as more than a mere physical body and to focus on developing the momentum of conscious energy as your main objective. It is not necessary, however, for you to embrace religion, or to accept any of

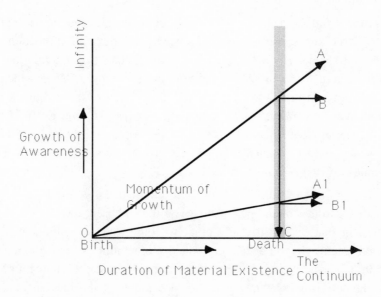

A = Continued Momentum Alternative

B = Personal Development Alternative

C = Material Survival Alternative

A has greater momentum than A1.

B has greater personal achievement than B1.

C has no effect after material existence, but shows that the one with the greater growth has more opportunity for fulfilment during material existence.

It can be concluded then, that there is no argument which

justifies passivity

Figure 5. PURPOSE TO GROW

our foregoing arguments in order to decide that growth, as an objective, is your only true course. You can do so by examining the alternatives.

First, from the perspective of our foregoing logic, you may accept that you are conscious energy which can develop momentum through the activity of addressing change. Second, from a religious perspective, you can accept that you are a spiritual existent which will enjoy fulfilment to the level you have achieved from your own endeavors. Thirdly, from a pragmatic perspective, you can reject all theories about that which you cannot measure and accept that you are only a physical body and that conscious energy will, in some way disintegrate with the body.

If you will examine each of these alternatives, you will realize that, regardless of the perspective you have chosen, there is no argument that will justify any objective other than development of momentum. If you accept continued momentum as your ultimate purpose or heritage, an objective of improved creative momentum is the only way to achieve it. If you accept personal achievement as your purpose, an objective of improved creative momentum is the only way of reaching your highest personal achievement.

If you accept that there is no purpose beyond material survival, it does not matter what happens after the body ceases to exist. There is, however, the necessity to enjoy contentment during the period of that material existence. Such a purpose cannot be satisfied without you growing to meet the demands of the material world as it continues to change and challenge you beyond your developed abilities to manage them. An objective of improved creative momentum, even just for immediate survival, is necessary. So, you see, it does not matter whether your ultimate purpose is defined. Your immediate objective cannot but be growth.

I wish to reassure those readers who may object to this argument as being a conceited effort to preclude the existence of a Deity by advocating independent growth. The common belief that the human being as an existent created in the same nature of the Deity, must pay respect to that Deity for our existence and objective is not necessarily disputed. Accepting this commonly held belief that the human being is created of the same nature as that Deity, it may be argued that such a Deity will also be the epitome of what you can determine to be the properties of the human being, only developed to an infinite intensity.

Such a Deity can be seen to exist if you can see that both you and I and many other entities like ourselves can exist to every conceivable stage of development without ever interfering with each other, each capable of growing from the assistance of the other without the other ever being depleted by the process of giving the other what he or she can use.

Then, it is possible that one such entity can be conscious energy with such infinite momentum that it will have infinite creative capability, infinite wisdom, and infinite contentment or fulfilment. If such a conscious energy exists and you wish to refer to that entity as the Deity, you will not have defined the Deity in any less manner than has been taught. The only difference will be that you will have arrived at your conclusion from the reverse direction.

In short, you may have accepted that the Deity existed because of what has been reported as Divine revelations, and because of the awe in which the apparent power in the measurable universe was held, and from that conclusion, that the human being had some special status with that Deity. Now, you can conclude that the Deity exists because we know of the special nature of the human being as conscious energy, and that it is possible for conscious energy to exist at infinite intensity without affecting or being affected by the spatial limitations observed of the material world.

If such a Deity exists as the fullest intensity of conscious energy, then, any attempt you make to increase the momentum of the conscious energy that is you will translate as a desire to be closer to that Deity.

If, therefore, your desire to be closer to that Deity causes you to grow, or if your aspiration to growth leads to greater closeness to that Deity, it really does not make a great deal of difference which is more correct. Either one will lead to the accomplishment of the other. Perhaps, I can illustrate this with a simple visualization.

You are in a race where the only apparent objective is a brass ring which is just out of your reach. Gaining the ring becomes the ultimate challenge. You run hard and you are able to get close to it. Yet, as soon as you do, something or someone pulls it away and you have to strive to reach it again. This continues for some time, striving to reach it, almost reaching it, and having it pulled away, until you became frustrated from your efforts. You sit down to rest, exhausted. Then, you realize something that was not apparent to you while your intent was so firmly fixed on the single objective you thought you had to meet. You learn that, in your attempts to strive for the brass ring, you have been gaining distance. You are much further ahead than you would have been had you succeeded in reaching the ring. As it was, you always had something to motivate you to go forward. Maybe it was that you really were required to accomplish the forward movement, or perhaps, it was that you were goaded into developing the strength to be more capable of using the brass ring when you acquire it.

We may never know if your objective then, is to use your capacity to grow in order to reach the fulfilment of being close to the Deity, or if the desire to be close to such a Deity causes you to develop the strength to deal with a greater challenge beyond your material vision.

Ingredients for Growth.

We do know, however, that if you wish to grow efficiently, you require two major ingredients. One is the challenge of something which requires you to create an understanding of it, something that challenges you beyond your developed understanding. The second is the fulfilment to fuel your creativity to increase its momentum and expand that understanding.

The first ingredient already is available in unlimited quantities, or at least quantities that are far greater than you ever can exhaust. It is the near infinite challenge from the constantly changing environment. Regardless how much you know, regardless how activated your momentum of creativity is, you can be assured that there always is more to challenge you, more than the tiny surface you have scratched.

The other ingredient is less available. It is the contentment or fulfilment from knowing that what you are is as good as or better than what you are expected to be. Simply, it requires you to be accountable for yourself. It comes to you only when you have shown that you have used your conscious energy for what it has been intended, to create new insight. Fulfilment confirms your value as a conscious energy, and gives you the fuel to continue increasing your momentum.

The only way you really can be sure of receiving this affirmation if you truly deserve it, therefore, is to have yourself judged for accomplishing what you truly can accomplish, growth of insight and understanding, an assessment which only you can make. You must be accountable to yourself as well as for yourself.

Being Self Affirmed.

If, as conscious energy, you cannot be measured with the instruments of the material world, it also is logical to presume that your momentum of activity and any growth in such momentum also cannot be measured. Yet, as you know, the activity of conscious energy creates insight and understanding, greater activity allowing for greater insight.

It is possible, therefore, to assess growth of momentum by growth of insight. You must, however allow new insight to be judged against past insight, and the usual way to accomplish this is through the expression of insight which then is judged against either a task or the comparative opinion of other people. There are three problems with this arrangement.

The first is that real growth in momentum is a factor of previous momentum. If previous momentum cannot be revealed, such a comparison cannot be made and you are judged only on the level of insight you have revealed. This may not allow appropriate recognition of the momentum you truly have developed. For example, you may have used your momentum to create insight along the lines of accounting. If you then are measured from how well you perform in medicine, you may appear, on the outside, not to have had any past momentum of significance.

The second problem is that an expressed insight differs from a true insight according to the efficiency with which you can express it. When your body, that instrument through which you communicate with the world, is functioning perfectly, you are able to express yourself at your best. The greater part of this problem, however, is that the body is rarely at peak efficiency. Constant change within that structure, and the need to train any form of expression, precludes any possibility that what comes out will be anything but a small fraction of what is meant to come out.

The third problem is that expressed insight is judged, either from how it applies to a task, or how an observer assess its applicability. As you know, the conditions that define a particular task change constantly. The insight, expressed to the task as it originally presented, may be inadequate for the new conditions that affect the task by the time the insight has been revealed.

When the assessor is another person, you also must remember the that other person may see the situation which activates your creativity from a different perspective. He or she then judges your expression by comparing it, not with your previous insight, a factor which may not be available to that person, but with his or her own insight. It is right, and you are effective, if your expressed insight is similar to or more extensive than that person's. Added to this is the reality that neither the person nor the task can be used to judge true insight, making such attempts to measure your momentum of conscious energy a predictable failure.

The only way such judgement of growth can be accurate is if you judge present insight against past insight, parameters that are accessible only to you.   In addition, as conscious energy similar to what every other person is, you are as capable of making an assessment as well as those others, one that is more appropriately associated with the level to which your have developed.

If you will accept that you have full capacity to measure yourself by your growth, and if in doing so, you discover that you possessed an inadequate understanding at a previous exposure to a situation, you also must have the maturity to realize that such discovery is a confirmation of growth.

The first insight was as well developed as you were able to have then. The second insight realizes the inadequacy of the first.

Therefore, between the two, there must have been further growth. Instead of being ashamed of your past inadequacy, you can congratulate yourself, not on how well you understand it now, because, if you have continued to grow, you will discover tomorrow that today's insight also was inadequate, but on having grown past what you understood yesterday.

This is the advantage of self affirmation, assessing yourself on the value of what you truly are doing, expanding yourself as conscious energy, the more developed that energy, the more valuable you are. The source of that growth is fulfilment. The only way you can acquire as much fulfilment as possible is to have a source which gives it for the most efficient measure of you that is possible.

Regardless of how much fulfilment you have, however, you are not using it efficiently if you do not divert it into fuelling your conscious energy. This means that you must be creative, and for that, you need to be challenged. Just as you can stagnate, and so lose

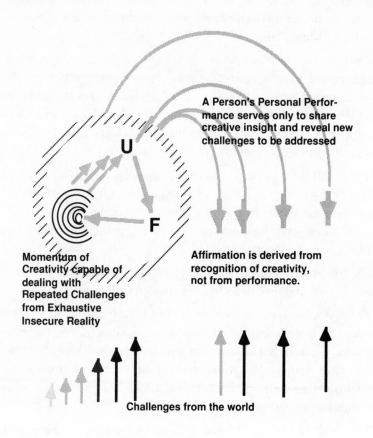

A Person's Personal Performance serves only to share creative insight and reveal new challenges to be addressed

U

F

Momentum of Creativity Capable of dealing with Repeated Challenges from Exhaustive Insecure Reality

Affirmation is derived from recognition of creativity, not from performance.

Challenges from the world

C = CREATIVITY   **U** = UNDERSTANDING   **F** =FULFILMENT

Figure 6. AFFIRMATION THROUGH THE RECOGNITION OF CREATIVITY.

significance as conscious energy if you do not get the fuel of fulfilment, so too will you stagnate if you have the fuel of fulfilment but do not use it to generate more momentum.

You need both. The world has one in abundance. To grow to your fullest potential, you need both in abundance. You need the other in just as much abundance. Do not also expect it to be given you by the world.

It is impossible for the world to be able to do it without having one offset the other. It is unfair to expect the world to provide each to you in alternate sets. This is done for the child. When you have grown up, you must take up your own cause, become a doer instead of a receiver.

The Advantages of Being Self Affirmed.

Because you are affirmed only when you use your creativity, an activity which is stimulated by new challenges and stagnated in stability, you will have the best opportunity to be fulfilled in an unstable world, a world of perpetual new challenges. Therefore, even though you will draw your fulfilment from yourself, you still will be humble, finding it necessary to keep looking for more challenges, for the opinions of more people especially if these take the form of constructive criticism, so as to keep expanding your momentum in order to continue receiving affirmation.

You will be better able to deal with the the realities of the world, seeing new problems as opportunities to develop your mind, not challenges to prove yourself. Your performances will be true revelations of your ideas, not investments to procure affection or recognition.

You will be able to accomplish because you feel good about yourself instead of seeking to feel good about yourself because of what you have accomplished, an attitude which lends itself to even greater accomplishments.

You will be more mature, a source of love and consideration rather than a needy dependent, draining it from those around you. You will be able to reveal yourself without the fears that you will show your inadequacies, because you will see inadequacies as revelations of where you can improve yourself next. You will see criticism as the consideration of the other person in reflecting your expression and so giving you the opportunity to improve it. You will be nurtured by what the world is willing to give you, change and uncertainty, not by what it has so little to give, recognition and affirmation. You will be able to receive as much pleasure simply from sharing as much as you do from being challenged because the act of true sharing forces you to create more insight to be shared, seeking more challenges to feed that creativity.

Hence, the more you give, the more fulfilled you will be, and the more able you will be to satisfy your purpose of activating and expanding your conscious energy. When you can use what the world is prepared to give you, the continuous presence of more work, as the opportunity for obtaining fulfilment, you will have reached the peak of efficiency.

Epilogue.

If you will examine all the things you see as strong, and try to determine what gives it strength, you will discover that strength does not really lie in power or size as much as it lies in invincibility. The object which cannot be destroyed is stronger than the one which can be destroyed, regardless of how powerful it may appear. The object which gains its strength from the weapons with which you try to destroy it gets stronger every time you attack.

When as a self affirmed person, you learn to use the challenges the world can throw at you, you too will be invincible. You will be unafraid of being destroyed as the weapons they use to try to destroy you are the ingredients you need to give you more strength. Just think. When you are promoted, you really are placed in a position of greater pressure. If you do not have the energy to conquer the new challenges, the promotion will show your inadequacies. If you have the inner strength to use the new challenges as inputs to your creative talents, you will become more capable than you were before the promotion. You will be strong. When you accept that the unknowns the world uses to manipulate you are only new challenges to stimulate your creativity, you will be immune to manipulation.

If you will examine the things that are weak, on the other hand, and try to determine what makes them weak, you will discover that the world can only weaken something that is vulnerable in the first place. In the case of the person, a true entity, that vulnerability comes only from the affirmation we seek from the world. The world can withdraw only what it was giving, leaving only what was there.

If the person had no other source of affirmation, he or she may appear to have been weakened by the action of the world. Just think. One of the most difficult adjustments in a marriage breakup happens to the person who is rejected by the other. If that person was already fulfilled, perhaps from another relationship, the rejection is less devastating.

If, therefore, when that affirmation is withdrawn, the person is left without any energy or inner strength, it is because that person was without it in the first place.

As a self affirmed person, therefore, you will be less affected by the withdrawal of affirmation. Because you are fulfilled from a source which rewards your creativity, you are less expectant of acceptance or recognition from others. There will be times when you will put yourself into a situation where you will get used to affection from an external source or need some. But these will not be as frequent as the totally dependent person will have. You will be hurt less. By having an alternate source, you cannot be weakened by the world. You will be able to rebound from whatever it does to you. Then, you truly are invincible.

As a self affirmed person, you will be accountable, independent, capable, and a true contributor to our common environment.

Chapter 7.

Organizing Your Management Skills.

Now that you are a self affirmed person, you will have a different perspective on your relation to the world. Regardless of whether the opposition is formed by the material surroundings, the people to whom you relate, or your own biological health, you will begin to see them less as potential contributors to your desired peace of mind, and more as weaker recipients of your organizational skills and administration. You will begin to see that what you do cannot be measured by the world as much as it is needed by it.

When those aspects of your environment are not managed by what you can do, you will see their response, less as an indication that your contribution is inadequate, and more as a recognition that you have the capacity to give more than you have been able to give so far. Any rejection of your management skills from any part of the world can be seen to be a request for better skills, more input from a source (you) which has been recognized as being capable of providing more management skills than any other inhabitant of this vast and varied environment.

The world is big, however. Its demands can go on forever. Therefore, no matter how capable you are, you must know that you cannot take on the world. But, the world does not know your limits. It, therefore, will come at you continuously, until those limits are reached or exceeded. This does not mean that you are expected to do all that is thrown at you, or die trying. It means only that you are given the opportunity to function to the level of your own personal limits.

The only way you can satisfy your personal objective of developing your conscious insight and fulfilment is by using your creativity. That means discovering your limits and challenging yourself beyond them. The way you can do that effectively is to organize your personally unique management skills if only to determine their limits.   In other words, you must have humility - the humility of knowing that whatever you have, no matter how great they may be, can function only within some recognizable limits. Knowing those limits means knowing how and where to extend them.

You must know too, that even after you define your limits, and even if you function beyond them, your contribution will be offered to a world that sees only those limits, not the assets that precede them.   You will not receive support or encouragement from the world for something it cannot see. Therefore, you must be able to get that encouragement from yourself. You must be self affirmed.

As a self affirmed person, you will have learned that affirmation can only be guaranteed when it is tied to creativity, your ability to formulate new insight beyond what you already have developed, and you need new challenges to allow that. Your management skills then, can either be a way for you to make a contribution from your more developed insight, or a way of removing the now redundant problem in order to reveal the next problem that will challenge your creativity anew.

The first definition requires that you have something to offer

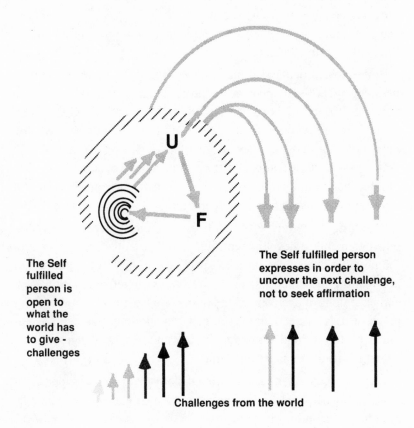

The Self fulfilled person is open to what the world has to give - challenges

The Self fulfilled person expresses in order to uncover the next challenge, not to seek affirmation

Challenges from the world

C = CREATIVITY   **U** = UNDERSTANDING   **F** = FULFILMENT

Figure 7. The Contributor

from a unique perspective, or one that has improved beyond your previous perspective. The second requires that you be prepared to use your creativity to analyze and understand the new problem that you will have unearthed.

Both of them demand something of you. They demand that you be independently charged for the performance of your duties. You now are recognized as having grown up. You are no longer a waif to be nurtured and groomed into a useful contributor because you now have reached the peak of your development. You can take your position as a member of the team. You now are expected to be able and willing to take charge of your own growth, further development, and degree of contribution.

In return, you will be given all the ingredients you need for you to reach your fullest development. As a child, you had, at best, half of the possible challenges because space had to be left for the fuel of affirmation, the other half of the necessary ingredients. Now, you can have control over one of the ingredients, affirmation, getting as much of it as you can allow yourself. In addition, you can have as much of the second ingredient you want, the challenges, taking from the infinite quantity available.

The only prerequisite is that you take advantage of that opportunity to be emancipated. You now are your own leader. You must be able to plan your own path, organize your own responsibilities. You must be able to examine the challenges made available to you and choose how extensively you will explore them, when you will take a breather, and where you will fix the limit for that particular area of responsibility. You will do this, all to the satisfaction of your primary objective of always making yourself into a more capable person tomorrow than you are today. You must take charge.

Taking Charge

A person who takes charge is a person who is strong, strong enough to consider the opposition, regardless of how wrong the opposition may seem to be. We indicated in the previous chapter that strength comes, not simply from how powerful you are, but from how immune you are to being overcome by the opposition. We also indicated that a strong existent is one which can, not only withstand the attacks from the opposition, but use those attacks as nutrition for its own growth. It is invincible because the more you attack it, the stronger it gets.

I am sure that you have been exposed to science fiction stories where the invader from outer space is seen as a formidable opponent, even if it does not attack us, simply because it is invincible to the attacks from our weapons, and because it thrives on the energy from our nuclear blasts.

.This is the ultimate example of true strength. This is a state which is fully available to you as a human being. The weapons the opponent uses are the changes that make your familiar conditions uncomfortable, and challenge the upward limits of your higher reason. They are the untimely erosion of a favorite object, the aging or injury to one of your body's organ systems, or the unexpected hostility from a previously friendly person.

The invincibility you have is your capacity to understand the challenge by growing as a result of its threat. Your only vulnerability is your need for affirmation, the reassurance that you are good enough to do what you are meant to do.

Therefore, the first requirement for you to be able to take charge and manage the events that challenge your management skills is to immunize the source of your affirmation from the forces of the world. In other words, you must not "wear your heart on your sleeve".

The world can only withhold from you what you have allowed it to mete out to you in the first place. You must not only have learned to be the most dependable source of affirmation, you must be prepared to be the only acceptable source. If, as a self affirmed person, you receive affirmation from the world, it is icing on the

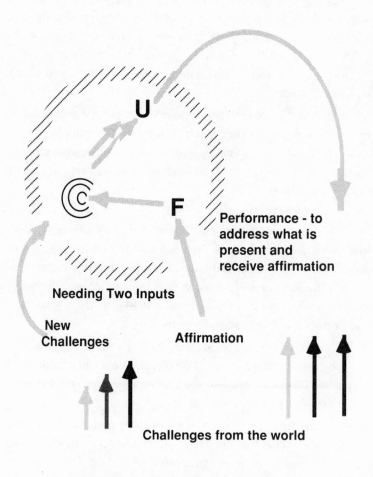

U

C

F

**Performance - to
address what is
present and
receive affirmation**

Needing Two Inputs

**New
Challenges**

Affirmation

Challenges from the world

How the Child Relates to The World

Figure 8. GROWING AT HALF THE OPTIMUM PACE.

cake. But for goodness sake, have a cake first.

The important thing to remember is that it is okay to get affirmation from the world. It is not okay to need it because such dependency places you at the disposition of the world in an area where you are most vulnerable.

We have learned in the previous chapter that you can assure yourself of affirmation simply by tying your fulfilment to the recognition of your activity as a conscious energy. All you have to do is to look at what you understand and compare it with what you understood just prior to taking on that responsibility. Even if you still do not understand the problem as fully as it is presented to you, the important measure can be satisfied if you understand a little more of it than you did before.

If, however, there is no enlightenment to allow you to feel good about your creative capacity, it may be because the problem is too different from the background information you have. This is comparable to a farmer trying to feel good about his ability to use a new deep sea fishing process. In such a case, you may benefit from doing a strategic retreat and re-examining a smaller part of the problem, perhaps from a different perspective. You may find also, that the acquisition of information from a more experienced source can provide you with the necessary foundation to progress at a faster pace. You can ask for help. Remember that other people are only too willing to express their perception of a problem to a person who seems to need it. Such an opportunity provides them with the reassurance that they may have greater wisdom than you.

Because you are self affirmed, the experience of exposing your relative lack of insight for that problem does not embarrass you. Rather, it allows you to get the other ingredient, the challenge, in a more manageable form so that you can stimulate your creativity and be fulfilled from its infused momentum. It prevents you from getting affirmation from an unreliable source while giving you all the ingredients for getting it from a truly reliable source and for a truly

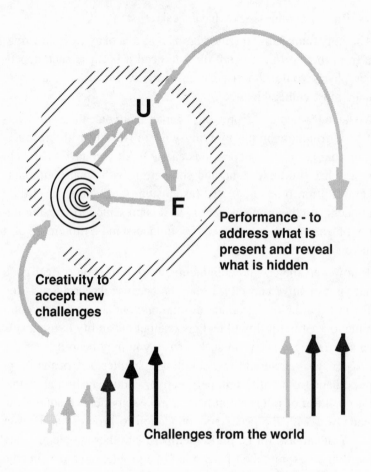

U

F

**Performance - to
address what is
present and reveal
what is hidden**

**Creativity to
accept new
challenges**

Challenges from the world

How the Responsible Adult Relates to The World

Figure 9. GROWING AT OPTIMUM PACE.

reliable reason.

If you already are in a position where you have drained whatever fuel you have so that you still cannot work on the newly acquired information, rather than go to the world to recharge you with un-earned recognition, you still can be fulfilled from the only dependable source, yourself. You must remember that the world prefers to have you as a source of organization and administration, not as the recipient of its good graces. The world resents having to stop to give you even a small recharge.

If you wish to understand this a little better, just think of yourself as the rest of the world to someone else for a moment. You, just as anyone else, prefer to associate with people who have a lot to give than with those who are seeking something from you. You may feel that way even if those other people rarely request your consideration. It may just be that they approached you at the wrong time. They may not know that you would have been more considerate at a different time. They only receive the message that you resent having to stop to provide for their needs. Yet, you may be one of the few people who are willing to stop and help the other person. This does not matter. What I am trying to get you to understand is not what should be, but what is available to you, as the recipient.

The way you can work on recharging yourself, then, is through looking back at your past accomplishments. First, you have to make a strategic retreat from the oppressing situation. Take a break. Then, you must look at what you understand now, not necessarily of the presenting problem, but of something which may have given you a similar challenge.

I frequently ask people, for example, whenever they feel that they are incapable of conquering a new problem, to think of the first time they learned to ride a bicycle. The idea is to feel affirmed for your ability to be creative, to rise above something that once was above you. By looking at the insight you have been able to create for something that once was difficult, you can respect that conscious energy again, and experience the fulfilment you need to energize you into working on the new information.

This, I believe, is the whole idea of prayer, not the penance of repeating a string of words, but the opportunity to reflect on what you have accomplished even if, to do so, you must be able to perceive that it has been affirmed by some powerful but invisible entity.

Therefore, the opportunity for you to be recharged does not just lie in your constant accomplishment in a thoroughly unstable situation, nor is it only available when you are forced to make a strategic retreat from an oppressing situation. Instead, you can incorporate it as a disciplined part of your day. As you become more used to doing it, you will be able to fall back on it automatically as a useful source of reassurance.

Another prerequisite for being able to take charge is to have a firm sense of purpose. You will have to become the only person to whom you can look for guidance and direction. Therefore, you must know what is your objective and why you are going there.

One of the determinants we have uncovered in our quest for the nature of conscious energy is that such an entity cannot be destroyed. Such an entity, we reasoned, cannot waste its opportunities at trying to secure survival, a foregone conclusion, but must have as its objective the determination to expand itself into realizing its full potential.

Your ultimate objective, therefore, must be determined by that need, the need to grow more creative, more insightful, and more fulfilled, the need to learn. Your immediate objective must be determined by your need to use as many of the opportunities that are available to grow, and to procure the ingredients that will allow that growth to proceed most efficiently.

The temptation is to reach a stage of development that will provide you with the conditions to to guarantee you peace of mind. However, as a rational being, you will be able to use the information provided in the foregoing chapters to conclude that no such conditions are possible. As a rational being, you must take the time to assess this and accept the objective of the maturity of your existence as a conscious energy, not just to win, at best a temporary state. Only then will you be capable of taking charge of your own relationship with the world.

The final prerequisite is that you must be prepared to use the opportunities constructively. You are going to be challenged whatever you do. If you do nothing, the old problem stays to haunt you. If you get down to it and solve the old problem, a new one replaces it.

Therefore, be hungry, not for the pleasure of the conquest or the peace of mind, but for the new problems.

The only way you can do that and enjoy it is by seeing the new challenges as ingredients to the realization of both your fully visualized purpose and your search for fulfilment. Your purpose is to develop your conscious energy, to grow. As a self fulfilled person, the fuel for achieving that comes from your recognition of its activity. Together, they allow you to need only one further ingredient, the challenges to stimulate that activity. You must want those challenges for your own personal development.

This may seem to be a selfish undertaking, one that is directed only at your own personal growth. Yet, we all are selfish. The human being is a self propelled individual. We cannot experience the insight, creativity, or fulfilment of another. Nor can we share what we have. We only can share what we can reveal. And we can reveal only as much as we understand. In fact, we cannot but reveal what we understand. Just by the act of applying our insight to a problem, we will have revealed whatever we understand of that problem, even if that application is made only with the intent of surviving the problem.

I am sure that you will admit that much of what you have learned from other people may have occurred without that other person knowing that you were learning from his or her actions or speech. Therefore, it cannot be selfish to try to improve that understanding if by improving it you have more to offer the world, and will do so automatically. If instead, you focus on your performance, you will discover that no matter how hard you try, you never can show more of yourself than what you truly have. However, the harder you try, the less that revelation will be.

Take, for example, the unfortunate problem of sexual impotence. The most frequent cause of male impotence lies in the man's attempts to measure himself by his performance, especially if the level of that performance is assumed, or is poorly defined. We will discuss this in greater detail under the chapter on stress.

Performance, therefore, must be a passive flow from you to the world. The acquisition of the insight which allows the performance is the active pursuit. Performance then becomes a simple revelation of your burgeoning insight, a gift you share with the world, not an offering by which you measure yourself. By being self affirmed, you can give selflessly as giving does not reduce you. It is only the overflow from an already fulfilled person.

If you can take charge of that objective of constantly learning, whatever you do will be a true gift, a true representation of a dynamically expanding and fully dependable resource. Because you know that your association with a challenge is to extract from it what you do not know, your discovery that a new task will reveal an inadequate performance will not threaten you. Instead, it will stimulate you, not to prove yourself, but to improve yourself and then share of that improvement.

Establishing Objectivity.

So you have learned to immunize yourself from the negative feedback of the world simply by recognizing that what appears to be negative feedback is really a recognition of your capability to be more creative and to manage more of the task with greater insight.

You have strengthened that immunity by accepting that feedback as the ingredient you need to stimulate your creativity, a momentum you desire. You have learned to be the source of your own affirmation from within to allow you to fuel your creativity and make full use of those challenges. Yet, despite emancipating yourself from the inconsistent assessment from the world, you still must emancipate yourself from you.

You must separate yourself as the creative entity from what you recognize as your ideas, the insight, which is the product of that creativity. If you will recall one of the rules which governs modern society, you will see how such objectivity does not conflict with traditional beliefs.   You must remember that modern society has evolved, in great part, from the teachings of Christianity, imposing conditions on you even if you are not partial to religion.

Much of the Christian religion is based on an admonition given two thousand years ago that we should grow past the previously necessary self protective regulations as, for example, the need to exact "an eye for an eye", and replace them with the new commandment that we should love God with our whole hearts and love our neighbours as ourselves.   Whatever you do, the acceptability of your performance is affected by how different people interpret this commandment.

The important consideration here is the definition of love. If you can see love as the act of respecting the existence of an entity, not as something else, but as that entity as it is meant to be, you will discover that your consideration of the differences inherent in that entity can be interpreted to be a manifestation of love.

The point is that, even if you consider it simply to be able to benefit from its differences, the same goal will be attained. On the other hand, any attempt to change it into something else as a prerequisite for that consideration, not only cheats that object from being what it is, but it cheats you from benefiting from what that object can contribute to your growth. Let us see how this can be applied to the three entities to which you are expected to give consideration, God, your neighbour, and yourself.

From our preceding discussions, you will remember that we have considered the human being to be a conscious energy which functions within a body, our purpose possibly being to evolve into a useful contributor to the world and to our own peace of mind. .As a result, we have suggested that what we believe to be the Deity may be a similar conscious energy, but one that has evolved to a stage of usefulness and fulfilment that supercedes all others.

If so, it is easy to give consideration to each of these entities without having to take from one in order to give to the other.   You can give consideration to any conscious energy by respecting the product of that conscious act.   As creative entities, we create insight. We share that insight either as opinions or expressive acts. The acts of the other people are their opinions that are expressed as their personal solutions for some common problem. Your acts are the opinions you form on the perceptions you have of those common issues. The acts of the Deity, then, must be those unexpected changes that are visited on us when we least expect them.

This presents us with a dilemma. How can we give consideration to an entity whose acts are in conflict with ours? Are we not then, required to choose one over the other? This is the dilemma which you have to face daily. Frequently, you solve it by making either a rigid choice, or indulging in inconsistency, giving consideration to one now, then another at a later time.

Some people choose to consider themselves. They see the unwanted changes in life as burdens that hinder their comforts. If they are religious, they may resort to prayer, asking for help to remove those problems. If they are not religious, they may use other means to be relieved of them. They may see the different opinions of other people as unnecessary issues that burden them and interfere with their peace of mind, frequently putting down these other people in order to elevate the value of their own opinions.

Some people choose to show consideration to the Deity.   They may accept every problem, every change, as burdens they must bear to show their undying devotion. They may do this at the expense of their own personal growth and development, or if necessary, at the expense of other people, believing that they are accumulating "Brownie Points" for their total disregard for themselves.

Some people choose to show consideration for other people. They place the opinions of other people ahead even of their own. They suppress their own opinions as long as there are other possible alternatives available. They act to help other people, not with their own solutions, but as instruments for the satisfaction of the expressed needs of those others.

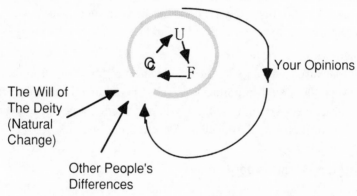

The Will of
The Deity
(Natural
Change)

Other People's
Differences

Your Opinions

Figure 10. Being Able to Show Consideration for all Three Entities.
(By seeing Yourself As a Creative Entity).

Yet, it truly is possible to be able to accomplish all three without resorting to inconsistency. Let us return to the definition of the human being as conscious energy. Then, you are not just your opinion. You are an entity which can create opinions.

Showing consideration for the Deity means being able to take the changes and unwanted problems as opportunities for your further growth. Prayer, then, if you are so disposed, will more appropriately be conducted as a request for the opportunity to show consideration, a request to be challenged.

Showing consideration for other people, then, would mean considering their opinions especially when they provide you with a different perspective, not just accepting those whose opinions are compatible with yours.

Showing consideration for yourself, then, means respecting your opinions of yesterday as good products of yourself as a creative entity, even though they may be different from those of other people, or inappropriate for the challenges of today.

Then, you can be the true creative entity, always being able to grow because you can give full consideration for the existence of the Deity, the equal importance of other people, and that of yourself, all as creative entities, their acts and opinions being only the products of their true existence as conscious energy.

Making a Commitment.

If you can see that your primary objective is the development of yourself as conscious energy, you will be able to see that it really does not matter what you have to experience in order to get the opportunity to create a new insight. In fact, it is less the particular experience that is important than it is the fact that you are experiencing something that you do not already know. That is the important thing, to be challenged beyond what you already know, not to be challenged to do the same repetitive task as a performance of what you know. This latter may benefit a series of observers or recipients. It is of no benefit to you.

As an example, if you leave a job because the work is too demanding, it may either be because there are too many new challenges that strain your capacities, or that there is too much repetition of the same performance that stresses your physical stamina and stagnates your mental capacities.

In the first case, running away cheats you of the invitation to expand yourself while in the second case, it gives you the opportunity to be exposed to more challenging tasks. In short, what is important is less what you do and more why you do it.

I have been able to use this logic when advising people in marital situations that are distressing. A woman who leaves a marriage because of a drunken husband, for example, may actually be allowing herself to be exposed to more problems in the outside world, but her creativity may be stimulated more consistently. Staying in the marriage may offer her a lot of challenges, but provide her only with repetitive demands. They may do nothing for her conscious development. If, on the other hand, she wants to leave the marriage because of financial hardships that she prefers not to bear, or because there is a promise of a more comfortable life with someone else, she may be cheating herself of the possible creative stimulation these challenges can give her.

Another way of looking at this is to state that you must be selfish, that is, selfish for the things that will stimulate your growth. Since the only thing which, as a self affirmed person, you need from the world is the challenge that stimulates your creativity, you can only be selfish for the challenge. As this type of selfish person, you will be the one to get up to do the dishes after a meal because such activity keeps your conscious energy strong and alert. As this type of selfish person, you will be the one to volunteer to do a difficult or dangerous task because you want the stimulation that the task will give you. This type of selfishness is the commitment that shows courage.

You, therefore, must have ahead of you at all times the realization that you are here to benefit by using the problems that are beyond you as invitations to grow stronger as a conscious energy. Since what is important is the problem that will stimulate your creativity, it does not matter what type of problem presents itself. It may come from the material environment. It may arise from the social environment. It may be part of the biological environment. By being responsible for your own growth, you are responsible for whatever of these that presents, not just for the challenges you want.

Your commitment, then, is to accept responsibility for your contribution towards all three parts of your total environment. Within yourself, you must be able to justify that total commitment, not just what is obvious to some partial observer. You, therefore, are responsible for your own personal health, your material surroundings, as well as your social associates. It is easy to believe that you are totally committed when you only are accepting one third of the whole responsibility.

The commitment to your physical task, for example, may appear, to the biased observers who need your contribution, to be the indication of a thoroughly dedicated person. The boss may commend you for your interest and dedication. Such dedication, however, can be accomplished only at the expense of similar commitment to the other aspects of your total responsibilities. In fact, it also may be accomplished at the expense of other material tasks as, for example, tasks that arise at home. You will be cheating yourself of the opportunities you can have from these other situations. Workaholics are known to neglect their own biological needs, or the needs of their families.

These other challenges can offer variety to your creative prowess, perhaps providing you with more growth than can be obtained using the same efforts to eke out the last drops from the end of an exhausted singular challenge. Remember that a hundred percent of one third is still one third.

You may choose, instead, to be totally altruistic, a people person. As a people person, however, you may expend all your efforts on the challenges presented by other people. You may receive quite a large range of challenges from this. You even may benefit from the experiences of all of those other people. You, however, will cheat yourself of the opportunity to have the variety that truly stimulates your creativity. To your friends, you may be a true hundred percenter. You are a man (or woman) of the people. Remember, however, the other person cannot experience your pains, discomforts, or stresses. The other person does not know of the tasks you may have left undone. You may be given a hundred percent for your dedication to people. Still, it is only a hundred percent of one third.

You may choose to be a health fanatic. As a health fanatic, you may pay particular attention to your body's nutritional requirements, its pains and discomforts, and its health. You may feel that your body will live forever, will never grow old, or will never experience stress. You may succeed at achieving one of these wishes for a short time. You will give little consideration to material tasks or social development. As a result, you will lose these opportunities to stimulate your creativity.

The challenges you can get from focussing on your biological health, the pains, discomforts, or stresses that are present to stimulate your creativity are multifold, sufficient to occupy your attention for your whole life. Just think, if you focus on the messages from your lower back as you sit reading this material, you may be amazed at the amount of information there is for you to discover and analyze. Yet, they were there while you were focussed on reading this material.

You do not have to be so focussed on them, however, that you will neglect the other opportunities there are for stimulating your creativity. Yet, some people do. They spend much of their time worrying about things that are inevitable with living, moving, and aging. These too, can provide enough challenges to occupy you if you want to grow only from the changes that occur within your own body, but they are, at best, one hundred percent of one third.

The point is that there are many challenges available to you. Your commitment is not to be totally dedicated to only one range of them. It is to the total dedication to the growth you can derive from your exposure to the whole range of them, the greater the jump from where you are to where the challenge takes you the more you benefit from it. The whole idea is that you must be committed to yourself, your own growth as a conscious energy. To yourself be true.

On your dying bed, you answer, not to your boss, your friends, or your aging body. You answer to yourself. If you can answer that you have used all the opportunities you were offered to your best advantage, then whatever you have gained is as much as you could have gained.

You will have done the job you needed to do in order to satisfy your higher purpose. If you have missed out on the variety of opportunities that you were given only because you were intent on being the specialist in one, you may discover that you will have missed the boat.

Organizing Your Time.

Now that you are willing to make a commitment to all three areas of your changing environment, you can easily become inundated if you try to take all the challenges from all the areas whence they arise. Remember that there is sufficient change in each area to occupy you fully for your whole lifetime.

You are the one in charge of attaining your objective, and you know you can do that most efficiently by being aware of all the opportunities that come at you. You can end up accomplishing very little, however, if you simply place yourself at the disposal of whatever comes at you. You must manage your commitment. You must manage your time.

Let us face it. Although each of these three categories of challenges can be seen to be distinct entities, so different from each other that what you do with one should not interfere with how you relate to the other, you may find that they are more linearly interrelated than such interpretation allows. What I mean by a linear interrelation is that each of these three areas of activity is dependent on the efficient function of the others for any of its challenges to reach you. Let us see how this happens.

As conscious energy, the challenges of the material world are brought to you by the efficient functioning of your body.   The body, however, can only bring to you those challenges that are close enough to stimulate its senses. Other people, on the other hand, can experience challenges that are far from your body's senses.

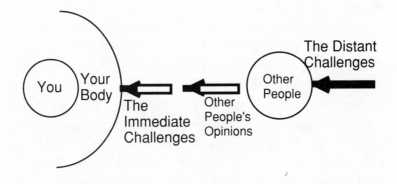

Figure 11. The Linear Interrelation

Therefore, people are needed to bring distant challenges to your immediate vicinity, either through the sharing of perceptions or through their activity in your immediate surroundings. Your body is needed to bring these immediate challenges to you.

If, therefore, you wish to benefit from as many of the opportunities to use your creativity as is available, you must recognize that whatever information reaches you flows to you in a sequential pattern. Each section requires the adequate function of the other sections in order that the maximum information can reach you. You must be able to use each section effectively. You must be able to take charge and consider your responsibility for the independent functioning of each area. You are the coordinator. Each area exists independently of the other. Their interrelation is only with regards to your connection with them.

Using your body effectively.

First, you must take care of the body if only to ensure that it is capable of bringing to you as much of the available stimulation that reaches it as is possible. The more efficiently it functions, the more information will be transported to you for your creative growth. Whatever challenges you must reach you through your body. If you allow the body to get too tired, or to burnout, the senses also will get tired. Then, what reaches you will be a reduced representation of what has been offered to you.

I like to draw an analogy here to a general of an army, you being the general and your body being the army. The senses are the communication media which allows the general to be informed of enemy formations and through which he reveals his battle plans. The front line troops report a particular observation. This information is sent to headquarters by means of a two way radio which also transmits new orders.

Somehow, the radio transmitter has been abused causing its decoder to function improperly. A new piece of information sent to the general becomes distorted giving a wrong translation. The general creates new orders based on the wrong information he receives. These are sent back, and again become distorted by the decoder. The solution which arrives at the front line seems so inappropriate for the problem that the general is thought to be incompetent. If applied, the solution may bring disastrous results.

In terms of the body, you must realize that abuse of it will cause you to have inadequate information on which you can work. Your poorly devised solutions will cause your contribution to appear confused, and perhaps lead to disastrous consequences. On the other hand, you may do the opposite and keep the body away from those challenges that can strain it. Then, you will have little to stimulate your creativity. You must remember that it is only those challenges that are beyond your developed understanding that can stimulate your creativity.

Therefore, it is foolhardy to abuse the body. It also is foolish to not use it effectively. The solution, then, is to balance its use and its rest. You must be willing to insert planned breaks, even if there is so much pressure from other areas of responsibility that it seems foolhardy to take that break. You must be willing to use your body as much as it will allow, even if there is the desire to stay in a position of rest.

If you do not insert planned breaks, your body will fail and an unplanned break will result, even if it is at the most inopportune time. If you do not use your body, those unused areas will degenerate or atrophy.

Many people who presumably are addicted to cigarettes or alcohol are people who also will admit to not having true planned breaks. These people will rarely, if ever, be found just resting at their desks for the short period of five minutes. Yet, they will stop to smoke, a task that requires a few minutes, at least ten times per day. They may stop for a drink. Then, they learn to associate that message from the body that a break is indicated as a desire for a cigarette or a desire for a drink.

The breaks provided by cigarettes, coffee, and alcohol.

If you drink, smoke, or simply drink coffee, just think back on the times when you experience the feeling for a cigarette, for a coffee, or for a drink. These feelings come at a time when you want to enjoy a break. You either have learned to associate the taking of a break with some act that excuses the break, or you have learned to associate the enjoyment of the break with some act that enhances such enjoyment. In the first case, what you will have demonstrated is that you have not accepted that breaks are necessary parts of working efficiently. In the second case, you will have revealed that you have not learned how to enjoy the simple pleasures that come with relaxation.

It has been said that cigarettes, caffeine, or alcohol have physically addictive effects. No real proof of chemical changes that can lead to addiction has been found. Sometimes, it is explained as an emotional addiction. Since emotions are not chemically induced, it is difficult to imagine the reverse, that they can initiate a need for a chemical.

If you indulge in any of these relaxing habits, do not be fooled into believing that you have no control over your desire for them. These are associated with a natural need. As long as you suppress that natural need your body has for a break, or as long as you do not know how to enjoy that break when you provide it, you will not be able to take that control. You cannot just stop smoking or drinking without also giving consideration to that natural need. It is impossible. It is this blind approach to stopping a self destructive habit that allows many people to fail in their attempts to take charge of themselves and use their bodies efficiently.

When to take a natural break.

Pay attention to your body. It communicates with you, and only with you. It cannot talk. It communicates by feelings. Those feelings are so personal and hidden that they have never been universally identified. Therefore, the way I perceive those feelings may be absolutely different from the way those feelings are brought out in your body. You will know them. If you smoke, they will be associated with the sensation of what the cigarette will do for you. If you do not have an addiction, they may be associated with an irritability, tiredness, lack of concentration, or some other experience that cannot be described, but which is either uncomfortable or worrisome.

From these discoveries, you will learn that your needs for a break can be affected by many external factors including the pressures of the work, health, level of insight, or state of nutrition. Each of these is so personally variable that only you can determine when a break is most needed and when it can be delayed.

Once you have determined the frequency with which a break is needed, and you have allowed flexibility for different situations, you will know when to insert regular breaks to reduce the degree of internal strain that determines when the body will indicate the need for a break. In some conditions, you will insert breaks more often than in others. In some conditions, you may insert no breaks, waiting for the expected conclusion to take a break. In some conditions, you will insert breaks that may seem unnaturally long to an outside observer, but which is appropriate fr your existing needs.

Then, your breaks will be natural, inserted not because your body desperately needs them, but because you have organized one of the things that is necessary for you to function efficiently, your instrument - your body. You will have been able to do this because you will have your ultimate purpose paramount in your mind - that of your conscious growth and development. You will insert breaks, not to be unproductive and lazy, but to be able to use your body more efficiently and develop yourself to your highest potential.

The insertion of breaks, then, will be a discipline that pays heed to the deeper discomforts while ignoring those that are less severe. It will be a discipline that allows you to continue to function fully by disregarding a discomfort you know to be associated with some chronic change that will not be reversed or reduced with rest, especially if it is less detrimental to your total well being than the consequences that will arise from inaction. It will be a discipline you easily can accept because you know that you will give consideration to your body without requiring a total shutdown to remind you of that consideration.

Sometimes, however, it is necessary to work for long periods without a break. Your body has the capacity to rebound from that as long as it is an occasional occurrence. Letting it happen too often can lead to severe burnout.

How to take a natural break.

Take charge. Since the factors that determine the need for a break are so variable and personal, it usually is unlikely that any observer will be able to understand why you may need a break at a certain time. That observer also may have a different method of taking a break. I am sure that you will be able to identify with this when you think back on one smoker telling another that he does not understand that person's need for a cigarette at this time. Similarly, a smoker who takes twenty breaks daily may think you lazy if he sees you just doing apparently nothing for five minutes. You, therefore, must know your objective and know that an efficient approach to that objective is more beneficial to you than an inefficient one influenced by the comments of an observer who cannot know what you need, at that time, to be competent and efficient in your overall responsibility.

Be aware. A natural break is necessary in order to allow you greater efficiency. A natural break, therefore, cannot be justified if, by taking it, you will have neglected to deal with an urgent situation that proceeds to a disaster because of your untimely and inconsiderate withdrawal. Such a break will be followed by a greater problem which must be addressed with more effort than was required for the initial problem.

How to use a natural break.

A natural break is designed to allow you to free your body, temporarily, from the external pressures that strain it. On the one side, these pressures arise from the external environment. On the other side, they come from you, that is, the activation of the senses and muscles of expression by you, the conscious energy. In fact, more often than not, the strain arises from your attempts, those of the conscious energy, to gather information, express insight, or seek affirmation from the world. Since, therefore, you are the main culprit, you can reduce that strain by removing the need to be aware of your relationship to the world. This means removing yourself, temporarily, from the external pressures that stimulate and challenge you.

One way of achieving this is to keep your focus totally within yourself. During the period you allot for your break, you may focus on a memory, a pleasant thought, or a repetitious idea, as is done in some forms of meditation.

Perhaps, the most useful way, however, is to train yourself to be aware of the other less prominent messages you are getting from the body, messages that send out feelings which can be interpreted as pleasurable. You may, for example, train yourself to appreciate the taste of your saliva, a useful tactic if you want to stop smoking. Your saliva can begin to taste like cool spring water as it becomes less affected by the effects of tobacco. You may learn to appreciate the pleasant feel of air as you breathe.

In other words, you can learn to indulge in very simple pleasures. This, obviously, is an activity which cannot stimulate you for long periods of time. Yet, it can stimulate you repeatedly over different periods of time. That is the intent, to give yourself a simple distraction that will not usurp too much of your time and reduce your total interest in the task at hand.

This is not a technique for managing stress. In fact, it is a preventive technique. By training yourself to do it, you will allow less problems to accumulate and be stronger to do those that are immediately important. Then, you will reduce the incidence of stress related problems in two ways. First, you will insert regular breaks that will delay the onset of strain. Secondly, the insertion of regular breaks will allow you to be more effective over longer periods, accomplishing more, and being able to solve more problems.

Nurturing the Body.

You know that if you own a delicate instrument, you will be required to use it, rest it, and take care of it, providing it with the proper ingredients for nurturing its strength. You cannot appreciate something as useful as an instrument if you simply place it on a shelf. You must use it. You cannot appreciate it if you use it so constantly that it breaks down. You also must balance its use with rest. You cannot expect it to function efficiently even if you do both of those things in proper balance if you do not also provide it with the proper nutrition to maintain its strength. If your instrument is made of wood or leather, you may polish it to let the oils strengthen its fibers.

If your instrument is a more delicate life form as, for example, your body, you will take care of it by providing a balanced input of the nutrition that it needs to function efficiently. Your body may be a sophisticated instrument. Yet, it depends on the logic from you, the conscious energy for it to be nurtured properly. If you put the necessary proteins in your mouth, the body will absorb it. If you put cyanide in your mouth, the body will absorb it.

Your body is a passive recipient of your management skills. It will function for you as well as you have nurtured it to function for you. True, there are many things that can affect the function of your body over which you have little control. Yet, you have control over the environment in which these activities occur. Therefore, you have indirect control over many of these things.

First, it is important that you provide your body with a proper balance of the necessary building blocks of protein, carbohydrate, fats, and water. Many people feed their bodies purely by reaction, not by taking charge and providing for its needs as the more capable decision maker. You may, for example, eat on the run, eating only to stop the incessant demands from an empty stomach. You may eat while watching television or conducting a meeting. You may believe that these activities save time or increase efficiency. Yet, with a bit of simple mathematics, you will realize how much it costs. If you can accept that poor nutrition causes the body to function less efficiently that it normally can function, and that it takes only a small amount of your time to eat a balanced meal, you can conclude that eighty percent of eight hours gives less productive output than even ninety percent of seven and a half hours.

It disturbs me to know that many people will eat poorly and discover that they have gained weight or are too tired to function effectively. Then they will diet by eating just as poorly, only with reduced calories. It is important for you to know that your body needs to replace, with new protein, the protein that must be removed daily from dying cells. It needs carbohydrates as the fuel to effect that rebuilding. It needs fat for a great number of reasons. One is to be able to absorb some foods, like vitamins, from the intestine. Another is as concentrated storage of carbohydrates. Yet another is as padding in crucial areas, not unlike the function of grease in a mechanical machine.

Yet, people will eliminate fat from their diets entirely and wonder why they are not absorbing the vitamins they take by the fistful. They will eliminate protein from their diet and stay in ignorance as the body breaks down good tissue in order to get the protein it needs to replace the cells that have reached obsolescence. They may believe that they have lost stored fat when any apparent weight loss is due to the unhealthy loss of necessary protein. Then the body will function so inefficiently that their total management skills will have all but been lost.

It is important to labor on this area of your responsibility because, unlike any of the others, you are the only one who can care for it. You must decide what type of balance it needs in the type of nutrition you are able to give it. From this, you must establish a pattern that is specific for your body's needs, working with the sources of nutrition that are available to you. You also must not believe that you are nurturing it well just because you balance your meals if you do not consider the act of eating as any one of your main responsibilities and plan it into your day.

Overfeeding your body in the mistaken assumption that you are treating it well is as bad a management approach as are the attempts to feed it only on demand. Eating is a pleasurable activity. People do not only eat to feed themselves. Sometimes, you will eat excessively, just to enjoy the pleasure of eating. Sometimes, you indulge in the pleasure in order to counteract an unpleasant experience, usually one associated with rejection or lack of affirmation. This type of mismanagement is called bulemia. Obviously, if a person suffers from bulemia, the ideal management is not a diet. It is the development of immunity from the hurts from the world, the main theme of this book.

Yet, you must know that your body cannot use all the nutrition that you feed it above its needs. It must store whatever excess you feed it as fuel. It cannot store protein, but it can transform excess protein into carbohydrate and fat. When it next needs protein, it still must have fresh protein. Therefore whatever excess you may have fed it cannot now be useful to you any more than excess fat may be useful.

Your body needs protein. Its needs for protein are determined by how quickly the old protein is used and broken down. This, in turn, is determined by how vigorously the body may be breaking down, as in recovery from an illness, the healing of an injury, or the overexertion needed for intense physical activity .

In other words, you also must be willing to be flexible in your management of the food intake. Sometimes, when you are using the body vigorously, you may need to provide it with more protein, even if you are attempting to lose weight. Sometimes, when you are less active, you may determine that you need very little You may achieve this by varying the proportions of protein, fat, and carbohydrate. You may achieve this by varying the amount of non-absorbable fiber content of the total food intake.

Lastly, you must not knowingly poison your body. This is a strong accusation. Yet, if you smoke, you are introducing carbon monoxide, nicotine, and tar, among other things. None of these are useful ingredients to your body's nutritional needs. They, however, accumulate to poison it.

If you drink alcohol, you are introducing compounds that can be broken down and used by the body only to a limited extent. Beyond that level, you are poisoning the body. Remember, without an efficiently functioning body, you never will be able to benefit from those other linearly aligned challenges.

Communicate with your body. Listen to it. Consider its needs purposefully. No one can consider it for you, No one can know its needs. Your body can give its messages only to you. Therefore, no one else can deny it appropriately. Train it personally. Free it from the expectations of others. They cannot experience its limitations. Only you can know how far you can push it today. Only you can know what specific discipline it needs today in order to function efficiently for you tomorrow. Determine those areas and train your body to be more responsive where you need it. You cannot train it to do everything. You must, therefore, train it in the areas that are pertinent to your needs, not someone else's. For example, if you live in the dessert, training your body for mountain climbing at the expense of training it to survive the dessert just to satisfy a critic may be detrimental to your more immediate needs.

Using the Immediate Challenges Effectively.

Just as you have learned to manage the body so that you can benefit most efficiently from the changes incurred by your use of it, so too you must learn to assess and manage the material things that comprise those challenges so that the changes in these also will occur in a way that will allow the most efficient transfer of new information to you.

You know that whatever challenges you get will come to you because of the changes that have occurred in the material that forms
the immediately relevant tasks. For example, you will not need to
clean the house if dust and dirt had not gathered in it. You will not
need to mow the lawn if the grass did not grow too tall for it. You
will not need to balance your budget if nothing is taken out and
nothing put in. In fact, you know that there never will be any job
for you to do if change never occurred in the structure of the materials that affect you for you to have to restore these materials, or for
you to have to strengthen them against unwanted change.

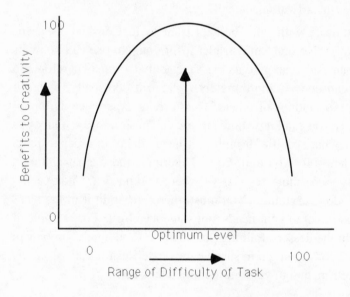

Figure 12.   An Efficiency Model.

Again, it must be emphasized that, as conscious energy, you have
an ultimate objective to stimulate your creativity to its highest potential. If then, a task can allow you to stimulate that creativity, you

owe it to yourself to accept that task and use it as a means of realizing your personal growth and development. If, however, that task becomes so great that your creativity is overwhelmed, the benefits you receive are as reduced as though you had no challenge from it. You must know when to use the task, when to rest it, and when to take care of the objects that influence it.

Using the task. (Facing Change)

It is universally recognized that whenever a task is not addressed, it remains to be done even as other changes continue to evolve beneath the surface of that task. These new changes may burst out and make the original task more difficult than it was. These new changes may remain hidden until you deal with the original task, becoming manifest only after that has been managed successfully.

What this means is that there always will be a problem to challenge you, the original one or the one that replaces it. If you fail to address the original problem, it stays to haunt you. Its degree of difficulty may increase, but the stimulation you get from addressing it does not. If you address the original problem, the next one that emerges can be more difficult. The difficulty inherent in any new problem, however, is such that your creativity will be stimulated to the extent that it is difficult.

In short, you will never have less problems as a result of procrastination. You will only have old problems with more work and no more stimulation than was associated with the original problem. With industriousness, you never will eliminate the work. You only will have more stimulating challenges waiting for you whenever you are ready to tackle them.

There are some tasks, however, which no longer challenge you. They once may have stimulated your creativity, but now change so completely within your range of insight for them that you can do well without having to address them. You know these tasks. They are the humdrum, routine tasks that you can do "with your eyes closed". It may be argued that since these tasks do not stimulate you enough to allow you to reach your ultimate objective of personal growth efficiently, they are better left undone, or perhaps given to another person to do.

You must remember, however, that by applying yourself to a task, you are able to manage the rate by which that task changes and evolves into some other problem. Leaving such tasks undone can cause you to have to attend to unnecessary work later. In other words, although the encouragement to keep your personal objective in the forefront may be interpreted as permission to forego responsibility for things that do not benefit you, it also can be seen that such a selfish interpretation can cause you to be inundated with unexpected work more often than it will give you freedom to do other things. The main objective of personal development can only be achieved through forming an intelligent approach to managing the immediate tasks. Procrastination and indolence can hurt only you.

Resting the task. (Accepting Change)

Things are going to change. You know that. You know that even if you manage a task perfectly, there still will be an area that will be beyond your understanding. You also know that you cannot manage everything. Some things, therefore, will have to undergo unpleasant change and you will not be able to do anything about it. Instead, you must learn to adapt to the new situation and live with it.

Surely, you will reap great personal benefit from attending to tasks that can challenge your creativity. On the other hand, you also will achieve greater personal benefit from a wider range of issues if you know when to stop your management of a particular task and go on to other responsibilities. Even though you may expect such a task to become more difficult if left unattended, you sometimes may find it necessary to offer what may be considered to be an incomplete management of it as your total effort. Only then will you be free to attend to other issues.

You have learned that you must contribute of your unique insight to all sections of the common responsibility, and in as many areas of each as you honestly can. It is easy to conclude, therefore, that you must be able to free yourself from some things and direct your attention to others even before you manage those things satisfactorily. You have learned that everything is in a constant state of change. Therefore, you know that whatever solution you may formulate for an existing problem cannot remove all traces of the problem. It serves only to reveal the next problem.

Perfectionism.

As a result, you cannot be any better organized by trying to complete everything to an absolute degree of perfection. The responsibility for tasks that appear from the material world can be compared to an impossible mathematical problem. No matter how much you remove from what exists, you still are left with all that was there before. You never can finish any task completely.

There is a story about Michaelangelo which is purported to have occurred before the creation of the David. According to the story, Michaelangelo was possessed with the need to create the perfect statue. No matter how he tried, some part would be out of proportion. He was very disappointed until one day he completed a statue of a male model. For the first time, he was satisfied with the proportions, and he felt he had made the perfect statue. While he was admiring it, a thought struck him that something as perfectly human as this, must be able to speak. He commanded the statue to speak, which, of course, it was unable to do. He became so upset that he threw his mallet at it and destroyed its knee, making it flawed and imperfect.

This may not be a true story, but it represents an important lesson. Perfection is a state which cannot be achieved. This is simply because what you may see as perfect at any moment is only the probable solution to whatever part of the problem you can see to that point. When you can apply that solution, it allows you to be able to see the next problem, and so on. You must know what can be achieved, and what should be left alone.

Overpreparedness.

You also must resist the temptation to extend your understanding of a problem so fully that you will try to manage all of it at the same time. You must remember that, regardless of how detailed your solution may be, whenever you reveal it, the relevant aspects of the problem will already have progressed far beyond what you were able to see as the original problem.

Perhaps an example is necessary. Suppose you have an exam or a presentation tomorrow morning. You may prepare yourself overnight by examining the problem as you see it in such extreme detail that it takes up an inordinate amount of your time. Then, at the time you are ready to present your solution, a new, unexpected twist is introduced into the problem. It may be a question from an observer who sees a different perspective of the problem. It may be that your solution can be applied so effectively that a new aspect is revealed, so closely tied to the original problem that the effect of your solution is dimmed.

When this happens, you are left wanting. You are too worn out to consider the new challenge. At the same time, you are seen as not having addressed the complete picture that now is more obvious to all observers. Although your presentation may have been prepared with great consideration for all the detail that was obvious to you, it is seen as an incomplete solution for what is now the immediate problem. Yet, having exhausted yourself in preparation, you do not have the strength to reassess the new problem adequately and create a more appropriate solution for it.

The only way, therefore, for you to know how far to go in addressing a particular task is to examine it with an eye, not only for the pure task, but also for other things that can be affected by it and which can affect it. There is little sense, for instance, in spending an inordinate amount of time polishing your shoes to a perfect shine if you know that you will be using them to dig trenches. You will polish them as well as they need to be in order to keep them strong, but you will be well advised to spend the extra time beyond that doing something else.

It is easy to do a task to the limits imposed by another person. Only when you approach each task, having educated yourself about more than is readily obvious, and being prepared to consider some of the repercussions that may arise out of your interference with it can you decide when you have managed it as well as it can be managed, and therefore, when you have done enough.

Nurturing the task   (Influencing Change)

Problems do not arise out of nothing. They come about because of the inherent changes that occur within the structure of the areas that form the task. Some objects or tasks undergo change more rapidly than others, creating new problems faster than you have the time to deal with them.

Yet, you can nurture those objects so that the rate of change that occurs within them can be made slower, or even faster than ordinarily will happen. Remember that whatever these tasks are, you share them with everything and everybody else. You are not the only force which can affect them.

Other forces may be the elements. They may be the actions of other people. If, therefore, you do not allot some time to protecting these objects, perhaps strengthening them to withstand more use than is immediately apparent, the next time you attempt to manage them, they may be so distorted from what you knew that they become an unnecessarily large problem to you.

Using People-Challenges Effectively.

Lastly, you must take care of how you relate to the people who affect you either at home or at work. People do not only represent challenges that are different from those you can perceive. They represent experiences that can stimulate you beyond the reaches of your limited senses. You must remember that your creativity is stimulated by the perception of a problem that challenges you beyond your developed understanding. Such perception can be evoked directly through the activity of a current problem. We have seen that it can be evoked from the activation of the senses even if no true problem exists to activate your senses, as happens when your senses are distorted. (drugs, alcohol, tiredness).

Such perceptions can also be evoked indirectly, from the experiences of other people. If you believe that you can grow to your fullest potential through your exposure only to those problems that confront you directly, you will be left wanting. You do not have the time. You never will reach your objective efficiently without also benefitting from the perceptions, and perhaps the short cuts to understanding their intricacies, that are available from the experiences of other people.

Obviously, too, you can get carried away and spend all of your time learning only from the experiences of other people. People want to reveal their opinions to you. In fact, they may even force their opinions on you. This is because people, especially those who are not self affirmed, want to receive consideration for their value as people. Therefore, what is available to you can be an oppressive amount of repetitive experiences, a detailed view of a singular experience, or a variety of new and exciting challenges. It is up to you to manage this source of information so that what you get from it will be useful to you and to your future contributions to the world.

You cannot dismiss what possibly may be useful to you without considering it. Yet, you cannot allow yourself to be inundated by all of the possible opportunities that can come from these other people's experiences. You must be able to educate yourself, even from the fool.

Using Other People's Perceptions Effectively.

We cannot emphasize too much that the world is multifaceted, and that it is vast. What is available to you is the whole range of activities that can stimulate your creativity. Yet, you are not able to experience all of them, simply because of the limitations of your reach. Even within an apparently simple situation, there are so many facets that one hundred people examining it at the same time, in the same room, will have one hundred different perceptions of it.

You can take, as an example, the act of sitting in a room with three other people. You may be examining the same piece of paper, but it is impossible for all of you to see it from exactly the same angle. Each person's perception will also be influenced by the presence of the other two people, a situation that is definitely different for everyone. More so, each person's perception is influenced by that person's past experience. How much you can see in a problem is related to how much insight you already have on that or a similar problem.

Each person, however, believes that what he or she sees of a problem is all there is to see because he or she cannot see any more into the problem than that. To each person, therefore, the other conflicting perspectives are wrong. If you do that, you will lose the benefit of the information that you can get immediately, but which you will have to extract from your own experiences at a later time anyway. If you behave immaturely, you will reveal your perceptions and become satisfied that you can overwhelm the opposition.

If you behave maturely, however, you will recognize that you must educate yourself on more of the problem than is obvious to you before you can make a qualified decision on your management of it. You will consider the other person's perspective, not as a competing opinion, but as one which may add to your perception of the problem. You then will have more information on which to base your decision. The other person may leave with the feeling that he or she has made a point, but without also considering yours, he or she will leave in no better position for managing the problem than before. You, on the other hand, will have left, stronger as a result of the confrontation than you were when you entered it.

Resting Other People's Perceptions.

Notwithstanding the fact that you need other people's input in order to stimulate your creativity and increase your capabilities, sometimes it is necessary to ignore what someone else is doing or has said. You must realize that you cannot learn from every aspect of every issue, nor can you remove all consequences.

You know that every problem is multifaceted, and as a result, there always will be other aspects readily exposed or easily aroused. You know also that these new aspects may have little bearing on the task as it pertains to the conditions that are immediately relevant. Just as in your management of the task, you have to know when enough is enough, there is a point in your relation with other people when you also must shut off their further contribution and be satisfied with the information you have acquired so far. Sometimes you must put a halt to the input even if you know that the other person truly has more information to share with you.

Just as it is inadvisable to be a workaholic or a self indulgent person, so too it is unwise to focus all your energies in pleasing other people by completely giving your consideration to their opinions. Therefore, you must be able to stop further input, even if you are pressured by the private needs the other person has for your consideration. You may be accused of being inconsiderate. You, however, have two other responsibilities which you also must consider, your task and yourself. Your job is to try always to be more aware, more informed on the widest possible range of conditions in order to make your best contribution to this world.

Nurturing Other People as Sources of Different Perceptions.

People do not always share their perceptions honestly. Sometimes they will withhold their opinions in order to give consideration to yours. Sometimes they will express false opinions, distorting the immediate challenges and making them more difficult for you to manage. They may do it from fear that they will reveal an inadequacy. They may do it in defense against your perceived displeasure. They may do it just so that they will not be challenged by you or give competitive information to you.

Yet, you need these different perceptions that the other person can share with you so that you can stimulate your creativity and increase your vision of the com-mon problem. You, therefore, must be able to nurture other people as sources of useful information, knowing when and how to draw out that information so that you can use it efficiently and effectively.

Feed their ego. Like you, other people are non-material conscious energies. What they need for nourishment is the feedback affirmation that what they are is good enough to be acceptable to the world. They need to know that their opinions are important. You cannot get much from a scared or defensive person if you send the message that what they will reveal to you will be treated with disdain. You must be honestly interested in the differences they will reveal, willing to consider those that seem way out, even if it means expressing an honest interest in exploring them further.

Sometimes, people are not willing to reveal an opinion that they believe may be upsetting to you. Shake the tree. If the lion comes down, it was up there in the first place. It is better to know the dangers that lie in wait for you when you are alert to them than to have them creep upon you when you are least capable of defusing them.

If you first immunize yourself by being self affirmed and being prepared for a new challenge, your early exposure of a new problem
will only serve to stimulate your creativity.

Lastly, whatever you do, you may not be able to obtain any information from the other people. Respect their right to privacy. Place
yourself in their position, You may be self affirmed, but they may
not be. They may, in fact be functioning in an insecure reality of
vast dimensions, so vast and varied that they will not be able to ascertain what may be threatening them at the moment.

Epilogue.

We have discussed your role as an accountable person, accountable to yourself, not just to survive - an objective which is destined
to defeat itself, but to nurture your own growth and development always into a more capable and useful existent. This is not a new philosophy of what should be. Rather, it is a realization of what is, and
an exhortation to be efficient through respecting what is, and fitting
yourself, the more flexible and expandable existent, into it.

There is much talk in business circles of the right fit. In social
circles, although the reference is not made to the phrase, the concept also influences our actions.

Getting the right fit, however, in its common interpretation,
means that the task or the people can be managed most competently
if they are compatible with the skills and understanding of the person who is responsible for managing or relating to them.

In this dissertation, we have attempted to show that such a right
fit is impossible, not because of the inadequacies of the manager,
but because of the constant change that takes place independently in
all three areas, the task, the other people, and in the manager's skills
and understanding. The idea is not to destroy the hopes of the
many people who look towards the realization of such a right fit either in their jobs or in their social and family relationships. Rather,
it is to proffer the suggestion that there is an alternative. Instead of

trying to force the impossible, or pretend that such a state does exist, you now are expected to be able to develop an awareness of what truly is happening, and use that awareness to your greater advantage.

This realization exhorts you to free yourself from being judged so that you can prepare yourself most efficiently to manage the problems that challenge you, problems that may not all be apparent to other observers. Now, you also must learn that you cannot judge other people. You do not know what priorities those other people have to consider, priorities that may not be apparent to you. You must, therefore, be able to function in your world and let the other people function in theirs. You must be able to relate to them without requiring either that they should follow your priorities or you theirs.

Chapter 8.

Performance Management

A capable person is only as useful as that person can reveal his or her capabilities. A person, however, is a self driven force. You are no exception. Your capabilities are as dependent on you as their usefulness is dependent on your ability to reveal them. We have discussed how to develop the management skills you need to let you manage the problems that challenge your capabilities. We have discussed how you must organize those skills to take charge of what you have to do, and do it. Now, we must discuss how to express those skills accountably. You must be responsible, not only for taking the initiative in managing the task, but also for the way you express yourself in your attempts to manage it.

Too often, you are led to believe that to be accountable, you must manage those issues that are apparent to any observer in a way that is acceptable to that observer. To be accountable under this presumption, therefore, requires that your performance be, not a revelation of the way you see the issue, but an expression that satisfies the way it is viewed by another person or other people.

This can be dangerous. The other person's view of the issue that you must manage may not be an accurate perception of what the issue truly is, or how it affects you. The other person may offer a subjective opinion, one that is influenced by that person's personal need, not by the pure needs of the issue. This makes your management of the task an irresponsible act, even if you presumed that you acted in good faith.

If you accept that, to be accountable, you must be accountable to some standard or representative of such standard, you still will be inefficient in all you do. You also could not truly be accountable. Let us examine why.

First of all, you are a self driven force. What you do is an expression of the way you see things, and things do change. If you must suppress your perception or the opinions derived from that perception so that your performance will satisfy an established standard, such performance will not be an efficient representation of anything. Your opinion, made for the problem the way it presents at the time, will, wholly or partially, be suppressed. The standard, made for the problem as it presented at a different time, will not be accurate for the problem as it presents at this time. Then, your performance will be irresponsible because what you do is a false representation of how you see the issue. You will have misrepresented your responsibility for managing the issue. You cannot then be accountable.

Secondly, you have a mandate to grow, to become a source of insight. You cannot allow yourself to be no more than an instrument - the arms, legs, and torso for the expression of opinions that are not yours. You must remember that your management skills are the tools you need to make you into a more capable person or one who has something useful to contribute to this world. They allow you to express what you are capable of doing so that you can go on to the next challenge and use it to make you even more capable. Just being the instrument for some other source of opinions is a misrepre-

sentation of your responsibility to yourself.   You cannot be accountable.

Thirdly, you may see a standard or expectation which places too
great a pressure on you to perform as being inappropriate for the issue as it presents now. This can cause you to disregard the importance of those standards or expectations. You then may express an
opinion that was formed only from the way you see the issue, or
rather than be considered incompetent in your performance, you
will reserve judgement and suppress your opinion. Then, you not
only will be inefficient, you will be misrepresenting your responsibility to consider the opinions of those other people. You cannot
then be accountable.

To be accountable, then, can only mean being able to be objective
at all times, considering the needs of the issue, and the needs of the
people affected by the issue and by your management of the issue.
To achieve this, the issue, and your management of it, must affect
you only as a creative consciousness, being the ingredients for your
continued growth and development.   To be accountable, then,
means being accountable to yourself, always willing to increase
your vision so that you, as a judge of what you do, can be, not just
the most appropriate assessor of your performance, but the one that
considers more of the factors that are pertinent to the issue, and
does so objectively.

Being Self Accountable

Standards and regulations are necessary for leading those who are
not self accountable, and for guiding those who are. The child who
is told not to cross the street has to follow a regulation. It is necessary for the child to be responsible to that standard because he does
not have the vision to understand the reasons for its presence. A
young adult who still follows that regulation is irresponsible because he has the ability to do more while still using it to guide him
in the way he manages the greater issues that challenge him beyond

those regulations .

Being accountable to yourself, then, does not mean being unaccountable for the way your actions are influenced by the experiences of other people. Rather, it means being more than accountable to these other people's experiences. It means being able to use their experiences as a jumping board to propel you into having a wider vision of the issues so that you can apply your decisions objectively and appropriately.

Your parents, for example, may have had good reason to make decisions the way they did for the circumstances as they presented at the time, and for the information available to them at the time. Many people, respecting the successes their parents may have had in addressing those issues, attempt to apply those solutions blindly. Yet, you must know that an apparently similar situation may have significant differences that can cause those solutions to be inappropriate for you now. You, also will have grown to the same age now as your parents were when they made that decision, but with even greater experience, or at least, experience that is more appropriate for the situation as it presents now. A new solution, therefore, even one that is directly opposed to the one they may have used successfully, will be more ideal for the situation as it presents to you now than your parents' solutions can be. This logic is true for any issue.

The blind allegiance to ceremony as opposed to doctrine, among many religious lay people, for example, does not take into consideration those two factors - the limitations of the teacher's exposure, and the presentation of the challenge at the time. Ceremony and standards pertain to the meat of the problem and can be applied successfully by those who are not experienced enough to be self accountable. When you need to address the issue more accurately, you have to be able to grow past the limitations of ceremony and standards.

Sometimes, your determination to be accountable to opinions or rules that have been formed for you is not always caused by your own feelings of personal insecurity. Frequently, it is caused by a need for relief from taking responsibility for your actions. It is easier to face the unknown with the instructions from a recognized source. Then, if you fail, you still will have been accountable to a recognized measure. If you succeed, your accountability will have been exonerated.

As a self accountable person, however, you are required to take full responsibility for how your actions relate to the issue, and how they affect other people while you are attempting to manage the issue. You, therefore, must have the maturity to make a decision considering as much of the information as is available, the awareness to express your opinion knowing that it cannot address all aspects of the issue that are visible to all observers, and the maturity to accept and deal with consequences, not as measures of you, but as new problems to be addressed.

To be accountable to a more experienced person is neither wrong nor self defacing. It shows respect for the greater vision of that other person. To be accountable to that person while suppressing your own experience, just to prove loyalty, is not only wrong. It is self defacing and dishonest.

This will not mean that you will be exonerated from accusations of irresponsibility nor from the punishments that those accusations may evoke. You must know, however, that the fall from grace which accompanies accusations of irresponsibility cannot be as reprehensible to your true self as the real irresponsibility you will demonstrate by choosing to appear accountable to external measures while being unaccountable to the more appropriate vision you may have of the issue.

There are a number of requirements that the self accountable person must satisfy. There are an equal number of benefits. The greatest benefit to self accountability is the freedom from having to perform to a measure that you cannot honestly satisfy. This is because the most frequent cause of stress and its companions, failure and burnout, is your tendency, as a self driven force, to toy to perform to a measure which is different from the way you see the issue you are managing.

If you succeed in satisfying the accepted standard of accountability, you will have failed the way you see the problem. If you succeed in managing the problem the way you see it, you will be seen as having failed as measured by the externally observed standard of accountability. Because you have not succeeded in managing the issue acceptably either way, the pressures of the unfinished task will remain to haunt you. As a self accountable person, therefore, the freedom from this unnecessary pressure can be the best gift you can give to yourself in addition to the gains you will have made in your conscious development.

The requirements for self accountability are that you have the flexibility to adapt your performance as the situation demands it, and the ability to accept criticism of your performance or failure to discharge the issue completely, as mirrors that show you how your performance appears. Only then can you use it to be even more accountable to your own deeper purpose.

It is no good having the quickness to assess a changing situation and create new insights as it changes if you do not have the similar flexibility to adapt your performance to address the newly changed issue. It is no good having the accountability to yourself if you do not take the feedback from the observers as mirrors allowing you to observe your performance as well as any other external observer.

Be alert. Everything has a new presentation every time you are exposed to it. Be inventive. Yesterday's solutions are appropriate only for yesterday's problems. Be wise. The appropriate solution for any problem is no more than is necessary to nullify the immediately relevant presentations. The overkill is as dangerous as the under-kill. Be considerate. If your performance creates a greater problem for the other person, the effects may be disastrous for the other person and the consequences to you may be more than you have the resources to manage.

Knowing these methods of managing yourself in a changing environment does not mean that you never will be wrong. It only means that whenever you are wrong, you will be able to accept it as a natural part of life, and that you will have the resources to correct it.

Establishing Flexible Priorities.

In the spring of 1987, a tragic accident took place in Europe. It was reported that a ferry taking passengers across the English Channel hit a sand bar, and overturned, killing many of the passengers aboard. The initial explanation was that a door to one of the holds could not be closed.

A more detailed explanation was offered later. According to the international press, the events that led to the disaster were multifold, and were compounded by bad weather on the day of the accident. In order to understand this and the lesson that can be learned from it, you first must be made aware of how a ferry functions. You must recognize that this event is recalled with the benefit of hindsight, and of course, without the pressure of having to make a decision under duress. Therefore, there is no intent to make an accusation. It is offered as an opportunity to assess the benefits of being ready to establish flexible priorities.

It is common knowledge that ferries take vehicles and people across large bodies of water. What is not common knowledge are the problems that must be addressed for the apparently simple management of that responsibility. A ferry floats on water. Cars must be driven from land onto the deck of the ferry, a movement from a relatively stable base to an obviously unstable one. Naturally, a ramp makes this less difficult. The sea level, and thus angle of the ramp, varies considerably from one port to the next, and from one weather system to the next. In addition, the weight of cars as they are loaded causes the deck level of the ferry to vary, again affecting the angle of the ramp.

This variability is countered by having holds in the ferry which takes in water, so allowing the bridge (the administrative center) to compensate for these fluctuations with adjustments to the floating weight of the ferry. When it is empty, more water is taken into the hold. When the tide is high, it also is necessary to take even more water into the hold so that the deck level is lowered and maintained at a constant relative to the land level.

Usually, a ferry will stay in port after loading in order to flush the holds and return to a proper water line. This is not always necessary as, under relatively calm conditions, it is possible to pump the hold while leaving port, and close the doors before reaching open water. Apparently, because of austerity measures adopted to make the ferry-runs economical, this was the method used in the months prior to the accident .

This leads us to the whole concept of flexibility. On the day of the accident, conditions were not normal. There was some irregularity with tidal conditions making the water level four feet higher than usual. This required that a lot more water be taken into the hold to allow the ferry to be loaded. Obviously, with such unstable weather conditions, there also might have been other changes in areas that are less visible. With that in mind, it would have been advisable to reassess priorities and stay in port a little longer so that, at least, some of the additional water could be pumped out.

You may know what happened. The boat left the dock on schedule while the hold was pumped out as usual. Sailing so deeply to waterline, it encountered an unexpected sandbar.

The captain did, then, what was the most appropriate manoeuvre. He turned sharply. This caused the water in the hold to rush to one side and the boat to roll. Frantic attempts to close the door and force the water out were in vain as too much water still was in the boat. As a result, the boat overturned and a number of people drowned.

The human being is, perhaps, the most flexible source of solutions there is. No computer can read as many variables, have as great an accumulative insight, or create a solution as quickly as the experienced person. Even if a computer can do it nearly as good, it will be because it has been programmed to consider as many variables and store as many perceptions as the programmer or group of programmers can think of loading into it. As a human being, therefore, you should never degrade yourself by allowing yourself to become only the tool for the computer or for the decisions of people who are not as familiar with the new variables that pertain to the issue as you may be.

You must be able to visualize and consider the new demands of the task, consider the conflicting opinion from the other person, and consider the experience you already have accumulated in order to make the most appropriate decision for the problem as you see it. Then, you must have the maturity to accept the consequences with the dignity of someone who has done what he had to do as well as he could do it. This is not always respected by the observer. Let us, for example, re-enact the event of the ferry disaster. This time, the captain will have the foresight to reassess his priorities and be accountable to himself in his management of the task.

He would have observed the boat lying deeper to water line than was safe. He would have surmised that such weather conditions would have had unseen dangers that might more easily be precipitated with the boat in such an unstable condition. Then, he would have made the decision to defy orders from his bosses, and wait until a significant amount of water had been pumped out, and have the boat sitting more stably in the water. Because of his added precautions, he would have missed the sand bar. No disaster would have occurred. He would not have been honored by the passengers who would not have known what could have happened. In fact, he might have been fired for defying orders.

In other words, there would have been a consequence, whatever his action. Now, tell me. Would it nave been easier to face the consequence of appearing accountable (to his bosses) while being unaccountable to himself, even if the disaster had not happened? Or, would it have been better to be punished for defying orders while, within himself, he can proudly know that he did what was most appropriate? In the first case, in the absence of a disaster, no one would have known that he just did his job. In the second case, no one would have known that he did his job well, and accountably. The rewards will lie within his own self-respect.

As a self accountable person, you will realize that your responsibility lies in your ability to relate to all areas of the world that affects you, or which you can affect. Some of these, like the feedback from your body, is privy only to you. Your actions, therefore, must be taken with consideration for all pertinent areas. It makes no sense to be so concerned about acquiring experience that you run your body to the ground and so lose any further opportunity to acquire any more experience.

We indicated in the previous chapter that you receive experience in a linear fashion. We explained that this meant that you cannot gain by paying more heed to one aspect and neglecting another. Your total capacity is as efficient as any one of those three areas of responsibility can be. Therefore, sometimes, it is necessary for a self accountable person to do less of a common responsibility if there also is an important problem in another less visible one.

Perhaps, a simple example will serve to illustrate this need for flexibility, not just in the obvious task, but in the management of the whole range of responsibilities. If you have to make an important presentation, but are struck with a severe migraine headache, you may have a compound problem. You may assess that the presentation is important, and must be made on time, even at the expense of its accuracy, or you may decide that the headache is so severe that you will be unable to make a proper presentation while being so disturbed.

In the former, you will establish a priority that allows you to continue as planned. No apparent change will be observed except in the accuracy of your presentation. In the second, you will have rearranged your priorities to make your physical well being important in the planned sequence. You know that you will be able to discharge the problem better when the headache has subsided.

Regardless of which decision has been made, even if you already have changed the planned sequence, you still keep assessing all three areas, the task, your body, and the needs and actions of other people. You may discover that you cannot make the presentation with the headache even after a grand attempt. You may discover that the headache subsided earlier than usual, allowing you to consider making the presentation earlier than may have been anticipated.

With flexibility, you are in charge. No one will know why you have made such apparently strange rearrangements of priorities. No one need know. It is your responsibility to manage all that is presented at you. You are responsible for yourself and for how you do your tasks.

Begging off because of a headache does not allow the observer to make the decision for you. That person only accepts that, for whatever reason, you have decided to give priority to something else. You still are held responsible for your decision, regardless of how much information you offer the observer so that he or she can exonerate you.

Asking another person to endorse a decision with information gained indirectly from you is no more appropriate than asking that person to endorse the decision without information. Information so subjective that it cannot be verified is not really usable for making an accurate decision. Such an action only removes from you the dignity of being truly accountable.

Asking another person to create a decision based on information available only to you may provide you with a decision that does not consider the real importance of the source of information to you or the severity of its interference on you. You may be forced into a position where you definitely will be seen to be unaccountable if you then change your priorities.

Remember that no other person sees anything the same way you do. No one else has the same vision of consequences as you do. No one has the same effect from those consequences as you will. No one, then, can establish the priorities that are important to the greater efficiency of your overall contribution than you can.

Using Failure to Advantage.

You may assess a task perfectly, make a decision that is ideal for the level at which you can observe the task. You can express that decision efficiently. Yet, when you do, you still are unable to discharge the task as well as you believed it should be managed. Your best effort was inadequate. You failed.

This does not mean that you are inadequate. There are two considerations you may not have entertained. The first is that everything is in a constant state of change causing much of your well prepared solution to be redundant by the time you are able to express it. The second is that everything is so multifaceted that you cannot see all aspects of any task, regardless of how experienced you may be or how carefully you may have examined it.

Without those considerations, you could not have assessed your apparent failure with true objectivity. First, if you approach a task with the objective of sharing what you know, that is, expressing your opinions, in order to manage the immediate aspect of the problem, disclose the parts that are not yet visible, or influence its continued change, you will have been prepared to accept that there always will be something else that needs to be done.

You will have been able to realize that a new problem is not always a new problem. It may be the problem that you did not intend to address in the first place, having succeeded in managing the problem you addressed. I guess that I am saying that the first consideration in recognizing failure is to assess whether the failure is real, or whether it is the appearance of success in small doses.

If you succeeded in managing the immediate aspects of the problem, all your apparent failure will have done is to allow that part you never intended to address to become more visible. You will decide whether this increased visibility has given it new prominence. Then, you will determine what you will do. Your apparent failure becomes a complete success, the way you intended it to be in the first place, as a person who is accountable to your own greater sense of responsibility.

If you succeeded in exposing the hidden aspects of the whole task, you can use your apparent failure to allow you to assess the new problem, decide whether it is necessary for you to continue its management at that time, and do what you determine to be necessary. Your apparent failure will have given you the opportunity to have more information to feed your expanding consciousness.

If you succeeded in influencing the further change that the task has been destined to undergo, your success will have been complete. Even if there is further change, you know that, at least, whatever further change takes place, it may produce less problems than the problems which may have evolved from the unattended task. You will have influenced its direction.

Obviously, even if you have a realistic objective, you still could have failed because your actions may have had the opposite effect to what they were intended to have. Instead of dealing with the immediate problem and revealing the underside or influencing its change positively, your actions may have disturbed the existing problem making it more visible, or introducing consequences that made further change less controlled.

Thus, secondly, you may not have considered as many factors that influence the problem as you may have thought you did in your

formation of your solution. Your solution was insufficient. This is
not a condemnation of you as much as it is an invitation for you to
hone your observation skills, increase your respect for those other
sources of influence, and reassess the approach you took to formulating your solution. You must accept that you were not born perfect. You were not provided with perfection. You only are a human being with an opportunity to learn, to develop your
intelligence to what ultimate purpose remains only a challenge to
your logic or faith as was discussed in chapter 7.

These tasks are not tests of your development. They are opportunities for you to determine your level. I tell students who panic for
exams that they must realize that the examination is not set in order
to see how stupid they are. It is information for them as much as it
is for their teachers. The examination shows them where their level
is. It is for them what a spike is to a mountaineer, a method of fixing their position, a point from which they can plot their further
progress.

Failure is a necessary input for you to make any improvement in
yourself. It is only from failure that you learn. If you do not fail,
whether your failure is apparent failure or true failure, you cannot
grow, and growing is the only realistic objective there is to life.
Real failure, then, is not the inability to discharge a task acceptably.
It is the unwillingness to use the new information to improve yourself. It is the revelation that you neither respect yourself enough to
use the feedback to grow, nor others to know that your unaccounta-
bility leaves them with a greater burden. It is failure to be self accountable.

Under these conditions, other people must manage, not only the
responsibilities that you will not bear, but the consequences that
will be revealed when your performance serves to worsen the existing problem, irritate hidden areas that you are not prepared to manage, and unleash further change rather than influence it.

If, on the other hand, you will accept failure as an invitation that is given only to those who are seen as having the capacity to be more capable today than they were yesterday, you will see failure as a compliment to you, a recognition that you have more areas which you can develop. A truly successful person, therefore, always fails. Like Edison, that person can recognize that the thousandth failure is the ability to know a thousand solutions that will not work for that problem.

Using Criticism To Advantage.

Your performance is your action, as a self driven entity, to express your opinion or impose them on your environment. There are two variables which can affect this. The first is your perception. You cannot see everything that pertains to a common issue. Therefore, the opinion you create cannot be appropriate for every possible factor that comes out of that issue. The second is your expression. Your performance is an attempt to express your opinion. Expression is a function of your value systems, your learned language or behaviour, and your developed skills. It is obvious, then, that what comes out is not always an accurate representation of what you want to reveal, and frequently, even less representative of what the issue demands.

You need criticism, therefore. Criticism, properly taken, can save you from the extremely severe consequences that sometimes can be elicited if a performance is too inappropriate for dealing with the issue. This is objective criticism, the attempt to provide you with honest information on your performance so that you can adjust it to be more appropriate to the issue. You need objective criticism from an observer because, when you see your performance from your perspective, you always see it with the benefit of knowing its true intent, an awareness that can give you inaccurate information about what really comes out.

Not all criticism is objective, however. People can be so subjective that the main thrust of their criticism is directed either to get you to stop doing something that can disturb their comfort, or to condemn you for not being accountable to the same standards as those to which they adhere. It is important, therefore, that you are able to accept all criticism and get from it whatever you can use constructively. Subjective criticism is based on how your performance is observed to address the issue. It, however, is directed, not at your performance, but at you. Subjective criticism can be as useful to you as objective criticism. It is up to you, however, to be able to get from it what can be useful to you. You cannot depend on the observer to make that adjustment.

I can tell you, for example, that your management of a particular issue fails to consider an aspect which I believe to be important. I can tell you that you managed that particular issue stupidly. The first comment is objective criticism. It is tailor made for you. You have the information that can allow you to improve your perception, and so your performance. The second comment is subjective criticism. Yet, it is based on a similar observation and assessment of your performance.

You can handle this in two ways. First, you can expect me to be intelligent enough to know that I can comment only on your performance, not on your ability to understand the issue. This, however, is an unfair burden, not only on me, but on you, as it places you at the mercy of every other person, giving them control over the benefits you can receive from the criticisms they can give. Secondly, you can attempt to transform that subjective criticism into objective criticism. Probe into my reasons. Find out why I believe that you managed it stupidly. This may be an invitation for me to destroy you more. Yet, how much more can I destroy you? I already have expressed my opinion.

If I continue to support that opinion, or if I elaborate on it, I will be revealing that I do not have the intelligence to realize that I am insisting that I know something I cannot read, your thoughts. If, instead, I explain the reason for my opinion, I will be providing you with the objective criticism that will allow you to take advantage of my observation of your performance.

Of course, before you can take advantage of criticism, you must be strong enough, or secure in the source of your affirmation so that you are seeking information honestly, not just confirmation that you have done well. You also must be prepared to use the information you obtain from the criticism to improve your understanding, or adapt your expression of it. You must know your objective - know how to immunize yourself as was discussed in chapter 7.

If you think of it, the worse thing another person can do to you is to leave you to wallow in your ignorance, let you believe that your performance is adequate. Then, when you attempt to express that opinion again in a more difficult or unforgiving situation believing it to be acceptable, you will be unpleasantly surprised by your unexpected failure, or destroyed by the rejection that will accompany your performance.

The best thing another person can do for you, therefore, is to offer you a critical opinion. It may not always feel good. In fact, the initial reaction is for you to protect yourself by ignoring the comment. If you do this, you will be no better off than if you were left with no opinion at all. Of course, the most frequent type of criticism is subjective. You, therefore, must always be able to explore and consider every subjective criticism, even if you have to make a strategic retreat and lick your wounds before attempting to explore the conditions that led to the criticism.

Always be prepared to look at the two factors that can be adapted. Again, we cannot emphasize enough that you must know your objective. If all you want to do is to survive the situation, it may not be necessary to use the criticism. You probably will never have to deal with it again. You must remember though, that if it occurs again, you will be no better prepared than you were this time. You will have to re-experience either the failure or the criticism that tells you that your performance can be improved.

If you have your own growth and development as your objective, you will accept criticism as an ingredient for that growth. You know that your opinion on any issue cannot cover the whole problem. You know that your performance is, at best, a poor representation of all you are able to reveal. You know, therefore, that any criticism is more an accurate assessment of the areas of an issue that you have not addressed, either in your consideration of it, or in your expression of your opinions than it is a statement of the other person's prejudice.

Therefore, you first will consider criticism as a mirror of your performance, not of your understanding. This allows you to determine where your inadequacy lies. If it is in your performance, you can attempt to restructure it, again seeking the feedback of criticism to polish it. If it is in your understanding, you either can reassess the issue or take information from the person who, obviously, has a different perception of it.

Secondly, you will accept that you cannot address every aspect of any issue. Therefore, you will know that there is a point when you can accept the presence of the criticism without necessarily needing to consider its input. Then, you will express your opinion, knowing that it may not be perfectly acceptable to that observer, but knowing that it is as far as you are willing to explore it.

Assessing the Accuracy of A Critical Opinion.

There is a double variable that makes the contribution of a critical opinion more complex than seems likely. This is because a criticism is the expression of another person, a person just like you. If there can be a variation in both your perception of an issue and your expression of the opinion you will have made on it, so too can the other person experience similar difficulties.

Whenever an issue is made complex by the interplay of two sets of variables, the easiest way to analyze it is first to examine one with the other presumed to be stable, then reexamine it with the other freely active. This is something you do regularly. You measure the movement of anything relative to yourself with the presumption that you are still. Then, you introduce your movement to allow you to get a truer perspective of the other. We can do the same with our assessment of a critical opinion.

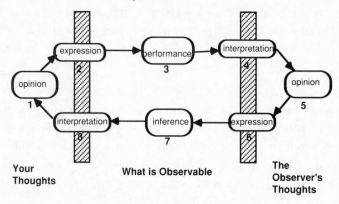

Your   What is Observable   The
Thoughts   Observer's
                                                          Thoughts

1 & 2 are the variables in objective criticism.
5 & 6 are the variables in subjective criticism

Figure 13. The Cycle of A Critical Opinion

First, let us presume that the opinion of the other person is an honest assessment of your performance, an objective criticism. That opinion then, acts as a mirror of what you are revealing of yourself. (In Figure 13, this is represented by (7) being an ideal representation of (3). Since you cannot see how you appear on the outside because your view from the inside is influenced by your knowledge of what you want to reveal, the mirror gives you an added advantage. You then have what can be an accurate assessment of how you perform. Now, you have two pieces of information, what you want to reveal, and what you actually have revealed. You can compare them.

If this feedback, a true measure of your performance, determines that your performance is inadequate, you know that its inadequacy is caused either by a flaw in your opinion (1), or a flaw in your expression of that opinion (2). If it is an accurate representation of your opinion, then the flaw lies in your opinion. That is, if (3) equals (1), and (3) is wrong, then (1) is wrong. You can reassess the problem using information gathered from the criticism to correct your perception of the problem or add to it.

Then you will form a new opinion, revealing it with the intent of reassessing your performance and, if necessary, correcting it again. If the feedback is not an accurate assessment of what you wanted to reveal, i.e. if (3) is not equal to (1), then (2) has distorted (1). You know that the flaw lies in your ability to express your opinion. You need to attempt to express yourself more accurately. Again, you can use information from the criticism to guide the expression of your opinion so that it is revealed more accurately.

Now, let us presume that the opinion of the other person is affected by that person's variables, a subjective criticism. The opinion, therefore, is not an accurate representation of what you did.

Before you can use this information, you must make it into an objective opinion. The person has expressed an opinion, not on the accuracy of your performance, but on its value. You need to know, not that your solution, for example, is wrong, but why it is considered to be wrong. You must invite that other person to be more descriptive in the criticism. You probably will be providing a forum for that person to elaborate, not on the reason for drawing that conclusion, but on why you are considered to be unable to formulate a correct solution. This may not be comfortable. However, the intent is not to accept that other person's determination of your accountability or that person's inferences on your capability at face value. Rather, it is to get information on those aspects of a problem you have failed to consider in your performance. Remember your objective - to grow, not to pursue survival.

You know that you cannot consider everything. You know that you do not always wish to consider everything. You know that you sometimes want to influence the change that you may see occurring in something. You know, therefore, that the feedback may not just tell you why you have been inaccurate. It also may tell you the limitations of the other person's considerations. Then, that invitation to the other person to continue to criticize you either will reveal new information to you on the subject, or it will reveal the limitations imposed on that other person by his (her) defenses.

With that information, you will be able to make an assessment, either of your further involvement in the subject, or of the importance which you will give to that person's criticism. In order to accomplish this, you must be able to disassociate yourself from the person's attempt to deride you.

You must know that the only thing visible about you is your performance, not your conscious ability. You must remember also, that as that conscious energy, your strength is not in what you already know, but in your ability to create knowledge. You cannot be condemned for not knowing. You only can be condemned for not trying to know. That, of course, occurs if you ignore the critic or silence the opposition without first considering whether he (she) has been objective in his (her) assessment. Only when you do that, only after you have considered that new aspect of the whole condition or the subjectivity of that other person's opinions, will you have earned the right to discount that opinion and proceed with the assurance that you have given full respect, both to yourself and to the demands of the task.

Sometimes you have to pay more attention to the critic, than to the one who unconditionally accepts your performance, even if that criticism destroys what you believe to be true. Just remember Hans Christian Anderson's story of The Emperor's New Clothes. The only opinion that was valuable to him was that of the child who honestly shouted that the emperor was naked while all his courtiers, in order to save their skin, lied about the fine texture of the invisible fabric.

Epilogue.

Even as you do these things, you also must be willing to enjoy the fruits of your labor. The admonition to be self accountable does not mean that you always must be working, that you always must be so self disciplined that your responsibility for relating to everything and everyone from the perspective of learning never stops, that you always must be looking only for the next problem.

It means instead that you must give account of yourself maturely, that you do what has to be done and be prepared to deal with the consequences. It means that you must realize that other people may not always manage maturely for their part, that their defenses will cause them to leave more for you to do than you ordinarily will be required to do, or even cause them to attack you for doing what you are prepared to do if it makes their responsibilities more demanding.

It means knowing that you sometimes will be condemned for your performance, but that you will use that to your advantage. It also means that your performance sometimes will be sufficient to deal with all the immediate problems that arise from a task. Then, you will enjoy all the benefits and pleasures that will come your way as a result of your successes. You will enjoy the comforts that you can derive from the material environment. You will enjoy your healthy body and all the pleasures it can bring. You will enjoy the satisfaction that compatibility with the people you have learned to understand can bring you.

You will do so, however, with an awareness that change is happening in invisible areas of each of these. You will enjoy them without becoming complacent and expecting them to be there always. Whenever the things you have earned to provide for your comforts are lost or become uncomfortable, you will accept that change as a natural event, and either go on to other things or deal with it.

Whenever you recognize an unaccustomed discomfort, pain, or

illness, you will not be surprised by it or panic because of it. Rather, you will see it as a natural event that calls for your attention to deal with an immediate problem and go on to enjoy new and different pleasures your body can give you.

Whenever the people with whom you have been compatible act strange or reject you, it will not surprise or destroy you. Rather, you will see their actions either as a message to you about changes within you that you can address, or as changes within them that allows them to be different, to accept different things. You will expect that their personalities will grow and will provide them with different perspectives. This will be an invitation for you to get to know more of their hidden parts, more of their new personalities, and to grow with them.

Stress, a problem in modern society, will be less visited upon you because you will have learned to use a fast paced world to advantage by adapting to the pace of these changes, accepting that, in doing so, you always will be the proselyte, always being willing to learn to do things because they have been presented to you, not measuring your worth by expecting that you already should be able to do what has not yet been presented.

Loneliness, a problem in modern society that occurs when you need the support or friendship of others will not be visited on you because you will be the source of support, not its recipient. You always will have what others want, the ability to give consideration and share understanding instead of looking for those others to share it with you and scaring them in the process.

Success, efficiency, and accomplishment will be easier for you to achieve because you will have learned to have a clear objective and the self accountability to reach it. Now, you must be able to share this with those who look to you for direction and assistance, or to those whose fears and defenses may cause them to burden you with their demands and frustrations.

Chapter 9.

Understanding People's Response to Change and Uncertainty

People are self driven forces. They manage a task independently. They must access their own skills and understanding. When they can access these, they do not need you to use them or push them. They can function adequately on their own. Frequently, however, they restrain themselves because of fear. The unknowns threaten to engulf them and cause them to fail. To lead them effectively, you need to know how to understand people and communicate with them, not only when they are willing to reach you, but when they are restrained because of their fears of the pressures within a task, or because of defenses against you or what you represent.

One temptation in managing or relating to other people when they are dependent on you to guide them is to use them as implements to accomplish your goals or to express your decision. Another is to expect that they should be able to manage without help, leaving them to be inundated by conditions that may be natural to you but

tremendously frightening to them.   Then you may be surprised
when their fears and failures encourage them to be defensive or
even hostile towards you or the responsibility you expect them to
manage.

What you need to know is that people generally are capable of
managing their responsibilities independently. They restrain themselves whenever they feel that the demands of the task will overwhelm them. When they are surrounded by problems that are
strange or unknown, they become afraid, and rather than expose
themselves to failure or destruction, they will resist, or seek help
managing the task.

As a manager, a person who has taken responsibility for guiding
your tasks towards a specific objective, you know that our present
era is replete with unknowns that reach everyone. You know also,
that these unknowns can cause problems even for you. It is not
difficult for you to understand, therefore, that the people who are
dependent on you will have even greater difficulty managing issues
that seem difficult to you, and also some of those that may be familiar or comfortable to you.

They will not tell you this. They only will use defenses that will
hide this inadequacy and protect their survival. What you need to
be able to do is help those people understand the task so that they
will manage it independently. With that, you will be useful as a
leader to the people who prefer the safety of the role of dependent.
With that, you also will be able to extend your reach as a manager
by using the resources of other people to manage a common task
more effectively.

You now need two ingredients to make this possible. The first is
an understanding of how the unknowns are generated so that you
can defuse the threats that evoke people's defenses and get them to
pull their weight effectively. The second is an understanding of the
defenses people use so that you can reach them effectively without
also threatening them further or inadvertently destroying those de-

fenses. You have learned to get the first. Now, you must learn to achieve the second.

The defenses people use to protect their integrity.

The most basic need of anyone, just as with anything that exists, is to survive. It is axiomatic that when something is destroyed, it ceases to exist as that thing. Inanimate objects have little choice. They do not have a defensive response. People, on the other hand, have a whole range of defenses. It is important, therefore, that people establish methods of defending themselves from the situations that may threaten to destroy them. Situations that pose a threat are those which have proven to be dangerous to a person's health or emotional well being. The unknown, because it can hide any type of threat is, perforce, the greatest danger to people.

The lower animals defend themselves by using the fight or flight response. As people, however, we exhibit a major difference from the lower animals. We are not just biological life forms. We are conscious entities. We think. What we use to drive ourselves is that conscious awareness, the energy which is associated with thought.

People, then, have two areas to defend, their physical bodies, and their conscious awareness. This may be termed a dualism of responsibility. To defend themselves from the threats of the opposing forces, they therefore must address three different areas of the conflict - the opponent, and two aspects of the self - the body and the mind.

Logically, there are three different stages in which people can establish these defenses.

The simplest way of protecting something from a threat is to remove the threat. In people terms, this can be interpreted as evading responsibility for the management of the problem, either through taking the person away from the problem or the problem away from the person. This is the simplest rule of nature, the fight or flight rule. This is the first stage - **evasion**.

DEFENSE TYPE	TARGET AND METHODS		
	OPPONENT	SELF	
		VISIBLE	CONSCIOUS
EVADE	Manipulate	Separate	Disregard
MAGNIFY	Possession	Position	Pretense
VALIDATE	Peer Values	Established Values	Personal Values

Figure 14. The Defense Systems and How they are Directed.

If the problem cannot be evaded successfully, the next stage in which nature logically allows its lower animals, and people, to survive is to scare away the opposition. Nature does it by providing certain animals with ferocious appearances. People can achieve this by magnifying their strengths. In either case, the intent is not to destroy the opposition, but to cause it to retreat. Usually, there is little depth to the strengths shown through magnification, but the opponent does not always know that.   This the second stage - **magnification**.

If they still cannot protect themselves from the threats of the problems, or if the problems just will not go away, they must face up to them. If these problems are so uncertain or so difficult that, even when they face them, they still cannot determine with certainty whether their management of the problems was accurate, it becomes necessary for them to seek to validate themselves. Validation can give people the message that they have accounted themselves admirably, or, at least acceptably, despite any apparent failure to manage the problem. This is the third stage - **validation**.

This separation into stages is an attempt to place defenses into a logical pattern. The stages are observed states. Some people can be observed to use only one type of defense. Some can be observed to use different defenses, adapting them to the situations as they need them.

This analysis of people's defenses and value systems has been offered to you, not for you to condemn them for the defenses they use, but rather, so that you will be able to understand when people are trying only to protect themselves. You must know that a person who is on the defensive is a person who feels threatened. Unless you understand this, you may perceive their defenses as attacks and do something which threatens them even more. Then, they will have little recourse but to defend themself even more.

When that happens, people can become so focussed on protecting their survival that they do not realize the new problems their defenses may be causing. By understanding the defenses people use, you will understand the level beyond which a particular person will have difficulty extending himself (or herself), and perhaps, how to help that person surpass that limitation.

The Simple Defense: Evasion.

The simplest solution to any situation in which the existence of one thing is being threatened by the action of another is to separate the two. We can observe this behaviour in people. However, even though the conflict may be seen differently from an observer's perspective, maybe even the person as the perpetrator, people still see themselves as the defendants and the other participant in the conflict as the opponent.

Since we are considering the defenses people use and not the right people have to exist undisturbed, we do not have to be concerned with the cause of the disparity. It may result because the challenge is too severe for a normally capable person, or that the person is too weak to deal with a problem that may be considered simple by any other person.

Regardless, the situation which exists is that a person's survival is threatened. To any person who is involved in a confrontation, then, that person is the target, the defendant. The source of the threat is the opponent, even if it is another person. Obviously, the other person sees that person as the opponent and himself (herself) as the defendant, but that does not matter here. We are considering only the defenses of the defendant, whoever that person may be. The fight or flight opportunity then allows the person either to separate himself (herself) from the opponent or fight the opponent in order to reduce its threat. As discussed above and displayed in figure 14, people have two areas of themselves to protect, the body or the visible self, and the emotions or the conscious self.

Using separation to evade an issue.

The flight response allows people to separate themselves visibly from the threatening situation. Some people may leave a job in order to take one that is less threatening, divorce a spouse, or avoid a colleague. Some people may give a responsibility to someone else. They may do anything that allows them to evade the problem by separating them from the source of the problem.

Using disinterest to evade an issue.

Evasion also allows people to disregard a challenge or the source of the challenge if it proves either to be too demanding for them or that it will disturb their emotional comfort. Some people will just explain that they have no desire to be involved with the problem. Some may ignore the presence of a task, or leave it undone. Laziness, or procrastination falls within this type of defense. Their main goal is to evade responsibility for the task without necessarily making their separation from the source of the challenge visible.

Some people may succeed so well in disregarding a problem that they frequently can live within a situation which appears totally unacceptable to any observer, without being aware that it requires better management.

Using manipulation to evade an issue.

The fight defense instead, allows people to achieve separation from the source of the problem simply by being able to manipulate or destroy the opponent. This is a frequently used defense, one that has been developed into quite a science. This natural defense uses physical or visible strength to counteract an opponent and so remove the threat. They will use whatever visible supports are available to augment their own strength, muscular strength, a loud voice, or even weapons, to outmaneuver an opponent's visible presence.

When the source of the threat is another person, however, people have learned to make use of their knowledge that other people too, are self driven forces who also must protect their own conscious selves as well as their visible selves. Their manipulations, therefore, can be directed at destroying the other person's conscious integrity, the ego, so to speak.

To tell someone that he (she) is stupid, for example, is a method of manipulating that person through weakening his (her) inner, conscious strength. To threaten to reveal a person's insecurities or failures, either to mutual acquaintances or employers or through the courts of law, can manipulate that person's conscious strength. Some people fool others into believing that they are weak, just to encourage them to reduce their demands, either out of consideration for their weakness or through the realization that these demands cannot be met.

You must remember that these defenses are revelations only that the person believes that he (she) is unable to manage the challenge satisfactorily, and is either afraid to confront it, or unwilling to get the resources to address it at that time. It does not label a person as an evader. It only can suggest that, for some reason yet unknown, that person feels threatened by the challenge of the situation as it exists, and chooses to defend himself (herself), at that time, by evading the apparently immense problem.

The middle defense: Magnification.

Nature allows its simple creatures the ability to counteract an opponent whose strength is far greater that that creature's simply by allowing it to appear more ferocious than the opponent. People do not have those assets. Fortunately, however, people's greatest opponents are other people. They, therefore, can put on the appearance of greater strength simply by appealing to the intelligence of the opponent. Then, the strength of the defense is as good as the perception of the adversary. They do not need frightening masks or fake muscles. People need use only the intelligence or the fears of the opponent to enable them to magnify their strengths and scare those opponents, or earn their respect.

Using pretense to boost one's image.

Take pretense as an example. Pretense is a defense that allows people to show a strength which they do not truly possess. This works only with adversaries who can ascertain the value of the person they are pretending to be, or the assets they are pretending to have. If someone pretends to have a particular skill, that person is able to fool other people only if they are sufficiently familiar with the skill to know the advantage it can give the person.

Some people may use bravado to show a confidence that they do not have. They may display a passing knowledge of a particular skill or expertise to suggest that they have full experience at it. They may offer solutions that are not theirs in order to encourage the presumption that they can do a particular task. They may lie, plagiarize another's work, or simply use the other person's ignorance to let that person presume that they have capacities they have not denied having.

Pretense wards off the source of threat if that source respects the strengths people are purporting to possess. It works because the opponents, other people, are intelligent. They know that, by suggesting that they possess a certain strength, the fears they can evoke within the opponent of a strength which that opponent cannot face, will be as great a defense for them as having that strength in reality.

If they can show their opponent that they are capable, not only of resisting that opponent's advances successfully, but perhaps, of having a stronger counter attack, it is foolhardy for that person to confront them. Unfortunately, it is a defense which can easily crumble if the opponent ever challenges it.

Using position to boost one's image.

Position is a more visible form of magnification. Its value as an asset is just as dependent on how well the opponent is exposed to its power as is pretense. Being the president of a corporate entity bears little weight if the other person does not appreciate the power which that position may carry. However, it is a tangible asset. It magnifies people by demonstrating visibly that they have achieved supremacy over a measurable challenge. The advantages are obvious. Not only can the people who have it be seen as strong, they can use that strength.

Position is gained by showing prowess in a particular field or over a particular group of people. Some people's position may result, for example, from having earned membership to an elite association. Some may have been elected to positions of authority as the result of a vote. Some may have earned the respect of a peer group for their skill at a task, for an act of bravery, or the like.

People in positions of power do not have to wield that power as a resource. If they do, it is only to appear stronger than they truly are, to exact respect, to enjoy a privilege, or to cower an adversary. Then, it becomes a defensive manoeuvre. Position gives power, but like pretense, it is a power that lies with the position, not with the person. The position can be taken away. Frequently, if these people have learned to rely on the strength of the position, they may not have developed alternative strengths. Then, as the defense crumbles, they may be left naked and frightened.

Using material possession to boost one's image.

Possession is another defense which can be used to magnify a person's image. A rich person always seems more powerful than a poor person. Possessions, therefore, can give the image of strength by suggesting that the possessor is capable of conquering the territory which allows the acquisition of those possessions. They are seen as the spoils of the victor, so to speak. This, however, does not usually require the same degree of intelligence to recognize its value as does either pretense or position. In fact, possession as a method of magnifying one's capabilities usually fools the less intelligent person or the person who does not have access to any other information on that person's true capabilities.

It is, however, a well accepted theory that people become successful when they appear successful. People, therefore, try to appear successful with the display of the trappings of success, frequently without actually being able to afford those trappings. Some people may visibly display their wealth or their unrestrained use of money. In modern times, for example, people have taken to wearing designer clothes in order to display that purchasing power. The emblems are blatantly displayed so that the level of the person's purchasing ability is suggested.

Some may display the ownership of certain valuable items like luxury cars, expensive jewelry to show that power. Some may make the statement with a particular address. These people even may expend more effort building up these assets than they do trying to increase their true capabilities.

The above observations do not imply that anyone who wears designer clothes, drives a flashy car, or becomes wealthy is using those possessions to augment his (her) personal strength. Possessions, especially of those finer things that make life comfortable, are to be enjoyed and cherished.

Possessions, however, when they are used to magnify a person's image, can be an indicator of how strong a person perceives himself (herself) to be. Sometimes the person actually can be more respected than the possessions allow him (her) to be. You can use it only as that indicator, a method of knowing that the person is not attempting to show superiority as much as he (she) may be attempting to defend an inferiority.

We live in an image generated era. We have learned to use images of success as methods, not only of defending ourselves when we feel threatened, but as ways of discouraging threats that are yet to surface. It obviously is difficult for a person to confront you if you already appear to have a strength that surpasses the challenge which that person is prepared to make.

Recognizing the use of such a defense, however, does not label a person as an image person. It only reveals that the person has extended himself (herself) farther than he (she) can manage at that moment. It simply may be a temporary reprieve. You must remember too, that these defenses are used by people who want to extend their reach beyond what they know they can manage satisfactorily, whether it is because they see themselves as smaller than they should be, or whether it is because they just want to be greater than what they are.

Then, when they are exposed to the more demanding situation that their ambitions bring to them, they sometimes become too afraid to face the full pressure of the expanded situation. At other times, they are unwilling to extend themselves to reach the new demands, and never intended to do so, only wanting the rewards which the image of greater strength can bring to them, not really wanting the strength or even the challenges of the new situations.

The most human defense: Validate.

Nature does not seem to provide the lower creatures with as many defense opportunities as the human being seems to have. Even in the simplest defense of evasion, they do not seem to have the advantage of being able to choose to separate themselves consciously from the presence of the opponent.

People, on the other hand, have those visible defenses, and more. They have the advantage of using their conscious awareness to assess danger beyond what is apparent and use it to create a unique defense manoeuvre. This, however, gives them the added responsibility of having to protect their conscious existent, or at least, protect its integrity.

If people cannot evade the responsibility for a task, and cannot discourage the opponent with a display of strength, they must be prepared to address the problem. This can be a frightening assignment, one that may display limitations that, hitherto, were apparent only to themselves. They, therefore, must have the ability to validate that what they can do is appropriate even if their management of the challenge shows significant limitations within themselves as conscious entities.

Validation is a way of defending one's honor when that honor is challenged by its own show of inadequacy. Validation can be used also to provide an apparently solid reference point to allow people the freedom to address challenges to which they acknowledge a personal limitation. Under this heading, we can see value systems as being the measures through which validation can be accomplished.

Validating through performance to established standards.

People usually develop value systems that have been provided by the people to whom they look for leadership and direction. In the most impressionable stage of childhood, these would be their parents. Parents may have provided value systems as established norms which they were taught, or solutions for problems which they experienced. This is an established value.

Established values obviously require that people learn from their parents the norms that are believed to be right. Parents, then, must have been taught those values, have the time to teach them, and the inclination to do so. Established values may take the form of religious norms, social standards, or family traditions. What is unique about them is that they measure the outward manifestation of adequacy. This fact allows people to validate their actions even if this performance may not be a true manifestation of their capabilities.

Religious norms, and the specific teachings of people whose opinions may have been influenced by the information available in a particular era, but whose interpretations are accepted blindly now, fall within this context. Some people maintain certain traditions that may once have been necessary to manage a problem that no longer exists. Some people force themselves into compulsive routines, just to satisfy norms, within whose limitations they believe that they must function.

When parents either do not have value systems they feel confident passing down to their children for their use in their different world, or when they do not have the time or inclination to teach the value systems they accept strongly, the children must seek validation from some other source.

In our modern world, especially as a result of the relocation that followed the second war, many parents had to bring up their children in societies that were as difficult for them as they were for their children. Frequently, therefore, these parents were so busy surviving in their strange environment that they did not have the time to teach their children the value systems they felt strongly about. Frequently, they did not have the inclination to provide value systems that they were discovering to be limited for their new environment or unacceptable to their new associates.

Sometimes, they taught those value systems nonetheless. Then, these children would have grown up validating themselves in ways that accentuated their limitations rather than allowed them to have some stability. Then, as adults, they may have had to reject these and develop a different value system, one that is based on their own successes.

The result is that, whether they did it as children, or if they did it later as adults, these people will have developed a personal value system, one that is based on personal experiences.

Validation through performance to personal standards.

People use personal values to let them be independent in areas that otherwise would have outmaneuvered them. By knowing that they once were able to succeed using that standard, they would be able to exonerate any subsequent failure as being due, not to their inadequacy, but to the circumstances of the challenge.

Personal value systems are limited because, like established norms, they may have been successful for a particular circumstance that cannot be re-enacted. Since they do not consider the newer aspects of present problems, they too are rigid, and reveal the limitations of the user. People do not always use past experience for personal value systems, however. They may use ideas formulated as theories within their own fantasies. They may use concepts that they believe to be right only because they have not been proven to be wrong as yet.

Such a person either continues to do things the way he (she) has succeeded in doing them in the past, or attempts to do them to perfection. The measures of completion, or the validation of accuracy lies within that person. What people who use personal value systems do not always realize is that everything is in a constant state of change. The solution which they used at one stage may still be adequate, but the problem may have significant differences that are not addressed by that solution. Then, their determination to apply that solution may alienate them from others who may be affected by their actions, or they may exhaust themselves trying to offer a perfect solution for a task which defies completion, a typical cause of burnout.

Validation through performance to peer values.

If neither established norms nor the opportunities to develop personal values are available, people will seek validation through their peers, peer approval. Of course, since the opinions of peers vary, not only by the differences inherent within each person, but also by the unique value systems each may have, and by the changes that occur within these values as these people grow, peer approval becomes a less rigid value system than the other two. This loss of rigidity, however, is offset by the corresponding lack of any form of stability. It causes a person to believe that one thing is correct one day, and be forced to replace that value with another that has greater appeal to another peer group another day.

Peer approval as a value system allows people who see their personal strength as questionable, to seek validation for that strength from an authority person, or from a group which becomes an authority because of the strength of their numbers. Unfortunately, the need for peer approval causes many people to exhaust themselves trying to satisfy the expectations of the many different sources from which they receive validation. The dancer frequently becomes exhausted while the drummers constantly are fresh.

Frequently, people who measure themselves by peer approval need to please other people so much that they will offer whatever they consider to be their assets in order to get approval or acceptance. These assets may be their ideas. However, more frequently, they find it necessary to offer their bodies in one way or another, their possessions, or their consideration.

People's of attachment to their chosen value systems.

If a person attempts to validate himself (herself) using any of the value systems he (she) chooses, you must realize that even if that value system may apear to you to be wrong, it still is a measure which that person trusts. That person trusts it more than he (she) does you. If, as the unwitting opponent, you attempt to show that person the errors in his (her) value system, you will be perceived as destroying what is near and dear to that person, the measure which allows him (her) to feel strong. If you succeed, you will have no more than a shell of a person as your ally. Usually, however, that person will see you as being a less enlightened competitor of the value system he (she) has been successful following in the past, and so reject you. In other words, whether you succeed or fail, you will have failed in your attempts to convert that person.

Instead, you must be willing to earn entry into that person's inner sanctum, the privacy of his (her) consciousness, a position you must be invited to take. You will be invited only if you are perceived to be safe. Therefore, you cannot approach a person carrying weapons of your own. You must be able to enter the arena naked, so to speak. You must be able to be strong enough to withstand that person's defenses without also having to resort to defenses of your own. In short, you must be able to immunize yourself. Only then will you be able to take the next step, that of managing those people or relating to them from a truly more mature position.

Epilogue

You must remember that the use of value systems, whether they cause people to be rigid in their views, or so wishy-washy that they cannot be dependable, does not define those people as weak or immature. We all use value systems whenever we need validation. Just because the value systems used by another person is different from the one you may be using, does not make that person wrong, nor you right. It only shows those limitations within which you, or the other people function.

I tell you this, not to show you how to exploit people's weaknesses, but to give a measure by which you can understand how far people can go without direction, and when they will need assistance or guidance in order to increase their productivity, improve their efficiency, or reduce their hostility. This is what you want to know about people in order to communicate with them effectively - the defenses they use when they are threatened. When you know this, and you know under what conditions they use them, you will have two important pieces of information. The first is how they reveal that they are being threatened. The second is the point at which they feel threatened.

The successful manager uses this information to relate to that person in the state in which he (she) is most efficient, his (her) secure reality. By knowing when the insecure reality has been introduced, it is easy to determine the outward limits of that person's secure reality at that moment.

You must realize also that the smaller a person's secure reality is the more readily that person needs to hide behind a defense. Therefore, the defensive person must be seen as the more frightened, less capable person rather than the person who is trying to attack or inundate you.

The important thing to remember is that it is not necessary for you to explore too deeply to establish why a person is using a particular defensive strategy. Instead, you must recognize its use and realize what that tells you. It tells you only that something is threatening that person, and that he (she) is functioning at his (her) limits. The threat may be a common responsibility, a personal experience, or you. It is your invitation to step back - allow that person the dignity of feeling safe the way he (she) has attempted to do so. Challenging that defense, or revealing that you know it to be a defensive manoeuvre causes that person to retreat even further. Sometimes, he (she) clings to that strategy more tenaciously. Sometimes, he (she) retreats to a more secure strategy.

Sometimes, you may approach a person with honest and good intentions and that person will respond defensively. It is tempting to react similarly and either berate that person for his (her) arrogance, or retreat and allow him (her) to wallow in his (her) ignorance. This may establish how wrong that person is to react so defensively to you. Yet, it gains nothing for you. All you will have demonstrated is that you can be as threatened by that person as that person can be threatened by you. Unless you can take the mature position and show that you can relate to him (her) knowing his (her) limitations, you are no better than the other person. In such a case, you are in no position to do what you felt you had the right to do - condemn that person's show of insecurity.

Take the mature position. Immunize yourself. Recognize that you unwittingly may have reached that person at a point of weakness. Then relate to that person within his (her) demonstrated limitations. Even if you have to apologize for something you did not intend, you still are freeing that person to be as effective as he (she) can be, and to relate to you more honestly.

This is not the complete picture, however. It is only the first approach, the attempts to earn the other person's respect. Until you do so, you cannot really be managing or leading the other person, be that person a child, an adolescent, or an adult. Only after you have reached the person beyond that person's defenses, can you influence that person into being more capable in managing his (her) responsibilities, being more independent, or growing to be more effective and efficient in his (her) duties.

Chapter 10.

Motivating People to Accomplish.

You are a manager. You know how to take charge and be responsible for the issues that affect you. You must know that, by taking that position, your advice and direction will be sought by other people who are not yet able to be managers. They may be your children. They may be your employees. They may be your friends and associates who respect your dedication and accountability, and who are unsure about their own abilities to manage the advancing unknowns. As a manager, the people around you will less be those who can give you direction and assistance when you are overwhelmed that they will be those who need to rely on your confidence.

Even as a manager, however, you sometimes will need the support and guidance of another person. That is okay. It is acceptable even for capable people like you to be weak at times. You know that this happens whenever you lose sight of your personal objective and use defenses that are destined to fall short whenever the going gets rough. You will have fallen back on these defenses because you are human. As a human being, you will fail sometimes and do things that your logic ordinarily will dissuade you from doing.

There is nothing wrong with having these human frailties. You know that. You already have learned to forgive yourself and rebound to take the helm again when you are required to do so. You also know that this tendency to fall back on your defenses happens whenever you feel threatened by something that is greater than your reason and inner strength allows you to assess and understand. Then, your immediate need for protecting either your physical survival or your integrity wins over any logic you may have developed. Then too, it is natural that you will retreat to the protection of your defenses and your value systems.

You have seen this happen to you. You have seen how long it takes you to be able to rebound from it even when you know what you should do, and when your logic tells you that you should not be concerned. You also have learned that you will have these moments again. Sometimes you will be forced to rebound from them alone. Sometimes you will have someone to whom you can go. This may be your boss. It may be a friend. It may be your spouse.

In fact, I believe that this is the real therapy of a good marriage. You have a spouse with whom you can enjoy a mature relationship when both of you are strong. When one is weak, the other may be strong. Your spouse can be the source of replenishment for you when you are weak. Then, when your spouse is weak, you may have the opportunity to be his (her) temporary source of strength.

You have learned to accept that it is human to fail sometimes, and that you will do so more frequently when you start being the manager, but less so as you learn to rely on yourself. You can see how difficult it is for you even though you already have some of the resources you need to be fully self accountable.

Now, you must consider those people who do not have half the resources you have. If you have had to retreat to your defenses as often as you have done, you will be able to understand that those people will have had to use theirs even more. There are many people who may have started life with so little nurturing that they have had to rely on their defenses from the very beginning. There are people who may have been provided with defenses or encouraged to use them with the erroneous assumption that they are the necessary tools for survival.

They may have depended on these defenses for so long that they rarely allowed themselves the opportunity to accept challenges and be expanded by them. Then they too will be forced to continue to retreat behind their defenses more often as they become exposed to more change. They, however, will do so without the benefit of knowing that there is an alternative, that they can take the helm and become managers too, if not of a full line of responsibility, at least of their own small area. While they do not know this alternative, they always will retreat whenever what they have to do seems greater than what they believe they can do.

For many of these people, their fears are more the result of them not knowing that they have the resources to manage the problem than they are due to an actual paucity of resources. Their attempts to defend themselves against the challenges that bring these fears, however, can cause them eventually to have a narrow secure reality. Then, the immensity of the pressures will become more real than imagined, and their stresses will increase, even under normal conditions.

Managing People - the challenge.

It is up to you to be able to help these people manage the responsibilities they have, if not for altruistic motives, at least for your own greater peace of mind. Your forward vision allows you to see more of the task that needs to be done. You, therefore, can see so many potential problems that, to manage the task adequately or influence its change, you must bring to the forefront more things than you possibly can do alone. For your own continued successes, you must be able to utilize the talents of these people without also evoking their defenses.

Secondly, when problems that you can see, but which these people cannot see, are brought to the forefront, either naturally or through your instigation, they will react to you as the source of the unnecessary problem. This will be an added responsibility, one that sometimes demands more immediate attention from you than the task did.

Lastly, even if you do not bring the problem but allow it to creep up on them, they still will resort to their defenses. Then, they may reject responsibility for the problem, or they will manage it so inadequately that you still will be faced with a greater task than was there before. Then, the mismanaged problem will be yours again.

For your own peace of mind, therefore, you must be willing to share your management skills with these people. You must accept that they too will be able to manage if only they will believe that what they can do is good enough to do what they have to do. Then, they will not need to resort to their defenses. It is up to you to help them expand that capacity, or at least, make the demands more equal to it so that they will function successfully to the level they have chosen to extend themselves. You may even be able to help them grow beyond those limitations and be more capable people who will take their place with pride in our common environment.

You must know also that some people do not want to have a greater vision. What they can see already frightens them. They are afraid that if they look further, they will be even more threatened. Some people may be so complacent with what they have been able to manage that they will not want to lose the existing status quo, and so refuse to consider any problem that may go away if they ignore it long enough.

If you want to be that more successful manager and either extend your reach further with the help of the people who can use your direction, or prevent any unnecessary work that may arise from their defenses against problems that they are not equipped to manage, you must be willing to include in your management skills an understanding of how to manage and guide other people.

Relating to people with the strength of understanding.

There are two factors to be considered when you are attempting to help a person manage. The first is the size of the problem. The second is the strength of the person. You must remember that your intent is to help the person, that conscious entity, to move beyond just surviving the problem and really manage it. Therefore, you are not concerned about shoring up that person's defenses. He (she) can do that better than you can. You are concerned, instead, about how what that person can do measures up to what he (she) has to do.

You must remember also that every person is a conscious entity. That person, therefore, must have the same objective of growth and development of creativity as you do. You also know that you can share your understanding and help the other person grow without losing any insight or momentum yourself. In fact, the mere activity of attempting to help another person gives you the opportunity to solidify what you know, or even extend it. Therefore, any attempt to help the other person manage by helping that person develop the creativity to manage, helps you.

You know also that the human being automatically uses what he (she) has been born to do, create insight. Yet, each person's momentum of creativity can become stuck or slowed down simply because, at a particular moment in its development, that person's conscious energy may have been inundated with too large a challenge. Then the person may have transferred his (her) attention to the development and use of defenses rather than be destroyed trying to succeed. In short, that other person is not necessarily failing because he (she) is stupid, lazy, or weak. That person is failing because the insight developed to date is insufficient for managing the problem as it is presented, and the momentum of creativity generated does not allow a quick enough assessment of the new problem.

This is a state which exists in all children.   It hurts to observe a child labelled as lazy, stupid, or weak when, by definition, that child is a person who has not yet developed the insight to allow him (her) to deal with many problems comfortably. That child has to be managed into accepting that he (she) can do the task.

This argument is the same for the adult dependent. Just because that person is in an adult body does not mean that he (she) has developed the insight for the problem or confidence in his (her) creativity as the physical development may suggest. You must remember that we are referring to the development of the conscious energy. That development is not coexistent with the physical development of the person. Thus, there is no need to label a person who is only showing a relatively limited insight defending his (her) survival or integrity as lazy, stupid, or weak.

Sometimes, that adult dependent is so only relative to the problem. In effect he (she) may be totally unexposed to that problem which, to you, may be simple, while being extremely familiar with a different problem that you may find difficult.   Unfortunately, however, that capacity to be able to manage a different problem often is not considered in the existing situation. Whenever this possibility arises, I always think of Albert Einstein as seen from the point of view of a fisherman teaching him the apparently simple process of fishing off the coast of Newfoundland.

The intent in managing the other person, therefore, is to accept that he (she) has the capability to develop the insight to manage the problem, but that, at the moment, his (her) insight is insufficient to allow an adequate representation to the demands of the problem. Whatever that person does to defend himself (herself) is less important than your realization of the state that exists. It is only with that realization that you will be able to help that person appropriately so that he (she) can give full account of himself (herself) and either extend your reach, or reduce the pressures on you, albeit less than you may have desired.

Considerations of effective management.

The first consideration, therefore, is that there is a real or apparent (to the person) discrepancy between what he (she) knows and what he (she) is required to do. Since people are self driven forces, what they can do is more related to what they believe they can do rather than what they really can do. This is the information you must use. It is information that is inaccessible to you unless you are able to have that person share it with you.

The second consideration is that, while that discrepancy exists, that person will be more focussed on defending himself (herself) from the apparent threat than in using whatever insight he (she) has to manage that part of the problem which he (she) can manage. In other words, you may get no output rather than the limited output that person believes he (she) can provide.

It is important, therefore, that you relieve that discrepancy. You can do this in two ways. The first is to reduce the problem. The second is to increase the person's insight. After this, you have to help that person expand his (her) insight so that you do not have to go through this process again.

It is here that your knowledge of people as conscious entities comes handy. You know that a person's insight is developed by that person's creativity, and that the creativity is stimulated by new challenges. You also know that the creativity, fuelled by the affirmation of his (her) capabilities, can be shut down if he (she) cannot rise above a challenge, and that this happens when the challenge is too demanding of the person. You do not know where in that chain help is needed. You, therefore, have to communicate with that person and gain access to that information.

There are, then, two areas where you can help immediately, and two areas where your help will affect the long standing productivity of the person. You may help the person for the reasons given above so that you can use what that person has to offer, rather than no output, and so that you can reduce the added problems that person can create if he (she) is allowed to proceed undirected. Yet, you still must be influenced by your knowledge that people are conscious entities. Their real value does not lie in their willingness to be extensions of you, but rather in their desire to do their part, give of their unique insight.

With these concerns in mind, you will see that the two areas in which you can help immediately are the areas where you bypass their creativity and help them equate what they can do with what has to be done. One way is to reduce the problem to be within that person's range. This can be seen as management by **facilitation**. The other is to increase that person's understanding of the problem. This is management by **education**.

You also will see that the two areas in which you can help the long standing productivity of the person are the areas where you stimulate their creativity. Since there are two ingredients to the stimulation of creativity, the fuel of fulfilment and the challenge of the problem, you must consider both in the sequence in which they can be more useful or less harmful.

The most delicate part of the person, and the one that is least developed in the person who is a dependent, is the ego, that person's self esteem. One way, therefore, in which you can stimulate the person's creativity is to provide affirmation for what the person can do. This may be called management by **affirmation**.

The other way, when you are satisfied that the person is not just weak, but is unwilling to extend himself (herself) is to delegate the task, allowing the person to be exposed to the full pressure of the problem or the consequences that may arise from the mismanagement of it. This may be called management by **delegation**.

The ultimate intent of any form of management is to help the dependent believe that he (she) is equal to the task, or is capable of

managing it comfortably.   The reason that management is needed
 is that the person does not believe that he (she) can survive the demands of the task.   The prerequisite for any form of management,
then, is to discern that the person is in a situation wherein he (she)
may be threatened by the demands of a problem, and to be able to
empathize with the person even if his (her) method of conveying
that message is by being irresponsible, stressed, lazy, or hostile.

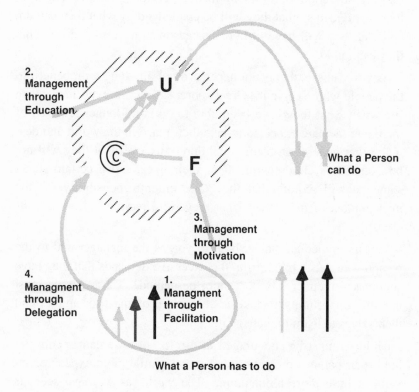

Figure 15. THE FOUR STAGES OF MANAGEMENT

Management Through Facilitation.

This is the simplest form of management. You do it with people, like children, who you know to be inexperienced and devoid of appropriate insight. You do it with people who are relatively inexperienced in a particular situation and who will not be required to deal with that situation very often, or ever again. You do it with people who are required to give special attention only to one aspect of a task, like members of a special sports team, or specialists in a particularly complex responsibility. Beyond what these people can do, they are not required, for the moment at least, to do more. The task, then, is divided so that they will be challenged by what they can do, and that they will have little or no reason to have to address what they cannot do.

As you can see, this is not necessarily of any long term benefit to the people who receive it. Great sports heroes discover this later in life when what they have been able to do is no longer required of them and they are expected to take their place in the world and deal with other general problems. Children discover that they will not be excused as children for all of their lives. At a certain stage, someone will require that they take fuller responsibility for the management of more than what they were required to do as children.

Yet, its immediate value, both to you as the manager and to the person who gets a break from the excessive demands that may have suppressed their creativity, cannot be denied. These people must use this opportunity to take a little more of the task and extend themselves to learn to manage it.

Children must be encouraged to use it, not to remain secure behind their parent's protection, but to get a little more exposure, develop a little more momentum. The world, as we have seen, is rough. The break a person gets when you facilitate them, is only a temporary measure. You cannot manage this way too long. As problems become more unstable, the parts you may have to do in order to facilitate your dependents can become larger until you become inundated with work that should have been accomplished by those other people. Parents who are too accommodating discover this long before their children become adults.

The point is that it is acceptable, even advisable to facilitate as a method of management. It allows you to get at least part of the task accomplished. It also allows you to have a base from which you can proceed to the next level of management. You, however, must use it only as a temporary measure, believing that people, even dependants, have the capacity to grow beyond what they know so that they can do more than they are capable of doing at the moment. Then, you must proceed to the next level, and educate your dependents to be able to manage more of the task and increase their share of the common responsibility.

Of course, you must proceed gradually. If not, by allowing too great an increase, you will revert to the previous situation where the other person needs to retreat behind the safety of his (her) defenses.

If this happens, it will be necessary for you to be the facilitator for that person again. Remove the extra part of the task. Delegate only that which the other person is capable of doing adequately. Remember, you can get more from people as self directed forces if they have the permission to focus on what they believe they can do independently instead of having to act as unwilling implements for the expression of your desires.

With children, it means that you must provide reduced challenges while expecting them to be a little more accountable every day. Too often, well meaning parents, afraid to hurt the child, do more damage through overprotecting that child from the challenges they are afraid to give them than they can do by challenging the child to stretch a little beyond what he (she) can do at the moment.

You must know, however, that you can cause just as much harm by stretching your expectations of any child without also providing ample opportunity for facilitation. In childhood, growing can be seen to be like walking up a set of stairs. The risers are short with gradually increasing heights. The steps are wide, giving ample time to savor the last rise, yet growing steadily narrower as the child continues to develop.

In the management of adults through facilitation, the same rules hold. Some adults may function at the level of children. This is not to discredit them. They may have been allowed to focus so singularly on a particular aspect of their development that, in the wide world of reality, they truly are children. Some of these people can be most respected for their unique knowledge in their speciality.
You must help these people when they become your dependents, even if that happens only for a short time, by facilitating their gradual exposure to the areas where you can lead them. The emphasis is on the firm but gradual exposure of these people by giving them only those problems they accept that they can manage while also attempting to increase those problems in small increments.

Management through education.

The next level at which you can approach the management of people, again with your focus on achieving an immediate balance between what they can do and what they have to do, is to provide them with information that is useful for their efficient management of the task. As you can see from the exact nature of the requirements, this already is becoming more difficult.

You are required to know what their specific needs are. Otherwise, you may be providing information that duplicates what they have while not satisfying what they need to know. This can cause the person to retreat more firmly behind his (her) defenses and to refuse to consider your next attempt to provide him (her) with information.

It is here that you need communication. You must respect what that person knows. You know that they know something. You only do not know what they know or how much of it is relevant to the issue at hand. The only way you can know is if that person chooses to reveal it to you, and that person will choose not to reveal it if he (she) believes that it will confirm an inadequacy which you may use to condemn him (her).

The rules of successful communications.

Therefore, the first rule in communicating with another person is to do so only if you can be genuinely interested in knowing what that person understands of a common issue. The second rule is to be genuinely interested in using that knowledge to help the other person expand his (her) insight. You can only be that genuine if you first have a good understanding of the task and the insight to show that you can manage it competently and confidently.

There is a third rule, and that is to be willing to consider that the other person may be reacting to an aspect of the task which you also do not understand, but which you do not see, and therefore, do not fear. Then, you must be able to be strong, not only because you have answers for that which you can see, but because you have the ability to formulate answers for that which is also unfamiliar to you.

If you do not heed these rules, and you show disdain for that person's understanding or retreat to a defensive position when he (she) reveals a greater threat, you may cause that other person to return to the security of his (her) defenses instead of helping him (her) become better prepared to manage the task appropriately.

If you wish to understand what may be troubling that person, you must be prepared to accept that he (she) is functioning in a totally different world than the one you can see, even as part of the environment you believe you may be sharing with that person. You must understand that he (she) will be taking the information you have given him (her) and applying it to a problem which you may not even understand fully, and if you do, you may not know the way it presents to that person, or what the consequences may be to him (her).

An adolescent, for example, may need to deal with a problem with his (her) peers that, on the surface, you do not accept as being of any great significance. Yet, you cannot assume that, just because you too have gone through the apparently similar stage of adolescence, your solutions will apply to his (her) situation. You have to realize that the solutions you may have acquired dealing with your peers may not work for him (her) just as his (her) solutions will not work for you in your situations.

Your world was not as compressed or deluged with information as the world of any adolescent tends to be. This, of course, holds true for any generation. The pace of change guarantees that the world of any tomorrow will be more demanding than the world of any today. This too, is as true for workers in a business. Similar problems do not challenge them in the same way they challenge management. In addition, they have to function in a different world from management.

You, therefore, must see that person's vision of his (her) problem through his (her) eyes. To get that, you must drop pretenses and show concern. You must drop disdain and show interest. You must drop fears and show confidence. No one can resist the opportunity to share the ideas they have formulated if they believe that those ideas will impress, or be useful to, someone who is knowledgeable and competent himself (herself).

In other words, you must show that you need their ideas. You cannot be genuine about that show of interest if you do not accept that the other person may have a perception of the issue that truly is different from what you can see, and therefore, can be no less important than what you know.

Now, with the awareness of the problem as it pertains to the other person, and with the willingness to accept that the solutions that may be useful to you from your perspective may not also be useful to the other person, you are better able to offer a solution that is more appropriate to that person's needs.

The simple formula for management through education is this: What the person has to do, minus what the person is able to do, equals the information you must share with that person. Only when you are satisfied that you have that specific information, and when you are prepared to share it as slowly as that other person's momentum of creativity will allow, can you truly presume to be managing through education.

Management Through Affirmation.

Now, you are prepared to manage other people by stimulating them to accomplish independently. You already may have taken care of their immediate needs, either through facilitating the task, or through educating the person. What you need to do in order to relieve yourself of the continued obligation to care for their immediate needs, is to help them access the strength to create solutions that are appropriate for the problems as these problems unfold before them.

You know that as long as the challenge is increased in small doses, and people have the inner strength to address the new parts of the problem, they can create the understanding necessary to deal with the task. You have seen to the first variable, first by facilitating the task, then by offering them information. The only requirement, if they are accountable enough to want to manage the task, is for them to have the inner strength to drive their creativity.

You cannot assume, just because some people have been successful, or because they have managed a difficult problem effectively, that they will know that they are capable. You cannot assume, because some people are receiving feedback about their successes in one area of responsibility, that they have the flexibility to extend it to their management of other things.

People may have knowledge and capabilities, but they may not always accept that they do. They still may be stuck in the cycle that requires recognition, acceptance, approval or respect from others in order for them to know that what they are is good enough to be what they can be. They need affirmation.

They need affirmation for their value as human beings. No matter how much a person wants to be appreciated for what he (she) can show, there is a burning desire within every individual to be appreciated for his (her) intelligence, his (her) ability to think and create solutions. The beautiful woman wants this. The wealthy financier wants this. The presidents and the governors want it.

It is for this feedback of affirmation that many people will display their visible attributes, or their developed insight, even if those assets they are offering have little to do with the problem they are required to manage.

It is up to you as the manager to recognize that, if you need your people to function effectively, you must be able to affirm them, not just for the physical strength or appearance, nor an understanding that is inappropriate for the immediate task, but for their ability to create new ideas and express them confidently. You must know that the asset you affirm is the asset that person will offer you. In a changing world, you need people's creativity more than you need just brawn or stamina.

You must be able to affirm those people for creativity, then. Even when they seem to want affirmation for less personal capabilities, you can be assured that you eventually will get more from them if you insist on seeking their opinions and affirming them for their ability to create those opinions. Yet, if they believe that they already have offered you their best asset, you will have to use it as the only area available to you on which you can provide feedback, prepared, of course, to encourage them to extend it at the earliest opportunity.

In other words, you must be willing to "prime the pump", that is, give the affirmation to start the creativity so that you will be able to affirm the effects of the creativity at your next meeting. You start by offering genuine appreciation to them for whatever they are willing to give of themselves, especially if you can determine that even a small part of it resulted from their use of creativity . It may be their best asset. It may be what they think you deserve to be given at the moment.

Earning people's trust.

You must realize that you are the one under examination. You are the one who is seeking to be trusted. If you want to get the most from people, and you do, you must be prepared to earn that trust and use it to nurture them to their highest potential. They cannot do it alone. If they could, they would not be needing your help now. If you are going to give that help, you must do so willingly and honestly. If you are not willing to give that help, you must be prepared to deal with the immense backwash that will occur as rapid change causes even the skills of the most highly trained people to become redundant in short order.

To earn that trust honestly sometimes requires that you make a comparative assessment against your own ability or that of a similar person. You are more likely to be believed if you can assure them that what they can do exceeds what you can do on that topic, especially if you are a person whose opinion they respect. Of course, you will be laying it on too thickly and lose that respect if you try to show that whatever they can do is better than what you can do. All they need is a reassurance that some little thing they can do is comparatively important. You must recognize that they already know that it is not great. Therefore, trying to elevate its value inappropriately may not work either. You sometimes have to convince them that their knowledge has some valuable applications, and use it honestly befors they will believe that you are not just putting them on.

Once you have started this, you must share further affirmation only for growth. Remember that is your primary intent. Do not lose it. Be prepared to expand your expectations, but do so in small increments. You can lose credibility if you affirm everything needlessly. You can lose that person's real potential for growth if you do not expect a little more the next time. You can lose your gains with the person, however, if you increase your expectations too rapidly.

Conversely, your credibility will soar if you can give affirmation honestly and appropriately. This is contrary to the theories of unconditional love. Unconditional love focuses on tying affirmation to the person's display of emotions, very subjective information. It does nothing for that person's growth. It only reassures you that you have help that person survive for another day, or maybe less.

This focussed management, perhaps liable to be called 'conditional love', has a specific objective, that of motivating people to become more capable and independent. For your own good and that of the other people, do not indulge in unconditional love.

You may return to facilitation if necessary. You may revert to attempting to educate the person. But give affirmation with a firm objective. If you give it just to make a person comfortable, you are not helping him (her). You are setting him (her) up for a tremendous fall. If you do it to earn that person's appreciation, are you not being the dependent and seeking affirmation from the person who needs it from you more urgently? If you do it just to earn your brownie points for heaven, perhaps you should reassess your interpretations of religion.

If after you have done all of this, those people still are unwilling to accept any more responsibility, only seeking repeated affirmation for a resource they may have acquired in the past, for attributes which they may have inherited, or for assets which they may have been given, you must be willing to stop giving that support. They may cry louder than before. They may accuse you of dishonesty. You, however, must accept that you have done you part. You have given them the opportunity to use the fuel you have so generously shared with them to stimulate their creativity and accomplish more.

You must be prepared, now, to manage them as people who are

too complacent to take responsibility for addressing the task, and who are satisfied getting affirmation for whatever little they can offer. They have been able to survive offering the barest minimum so far. They have always had someone to pick up the slack and cover for them. You must be able to manage above that. You, however, know that they only can grow by accepting tasks they would rather not do. You, therefore, are required to help them grow by giving them responsibility for those tasks even if you have to allow them to experience the full thrust of the consequences which the mismanagement of that task will evoke.

Management Through Delegation.

You have helped people by making their responsibilities easier. You have shared the insight and understanding that is yours so that they can escape the tremendous pressures that can shut down a poorly developed creativity. You have given them the encouragement and appreciation they may have needed to restart that creative momentum. You must know when you can do no more.

There will come a time when they must be encouraged to shoulder their own responsibilities and deal with the consequences. The worse thing you can do for them, and you, at this stage, is to continue carrying them. You must let them face the real consequences. They must be allowed to face the pressures and know what is required of them. This is the only way you can respect people as real human beings. If not, you will be treating them as less than human, as machines that can do no more than you give them the fuel to do.

If, however, a person prefers to be protected, to be given the solutions, and is satisfied just being a tool for you or for any other manager despite your attempts to stimulate his (her) growth, there is very little more you can do. That person will have chosen his (her) path. You, at least, will have tried. There will be no need to advance your management of that person to the level of delegation. Then, your management will revert to that of facilitation. You cannot continue to educate or affirm a person who is unwilling to take the reins and go for himself (herself).

Sometimes, however, you cannot give up, either because the person still will be there leaving his (her) responsibilities undone, or because it is a child for whom you cannot relinquish your responsibility. You need to help that person be a person by taking responsibility for causing that person to grow beyond what he (she) seems to have decided to accept.

Sadly, many of these people can continue doing only as much as they need to do just to survive because there always will be someone to buffer their consequences in the mistaken assumption that they are saving that person from experiencing a severe discomfort. Instead, they are only succeeding in stagnating that person's growth.

I remember a person who spent over two years trying to help a woman get a special subsidized apartment because she was afraid that her ex-husband might harm her. This person felt that this girl's need was serious because she was able to convince him that she truly was afraid for her life. In the end, he failed. When he did, the girl had little choice but to go out on her own and get a job to pay for her own apartment. By doing so, she was able to do for herself what another person would have prevented her from doing - being responsible for herself. Eventually, she met someone and remarried. This may not have happened had he succeeded in stagnating that girl in his attempts to overprotect her.

In the case of a child, other adults or society in general will unwittingly overprotect that child out of fear that he (she) is unable to think or create solutions for complex problems. With the other adult, it is the person who knows how to get sympathy that usually cries the loudest. It is the one who cries the loudest that who will convince people that he (she) is the most needy. .i.Manipulation; This is a form of defense through manipulation. As that person is able to succeed in using the manipulative defense, the relative strength of his (her) secure reality will diminish, and he (she) will be threatened by more of the natural events that will have evolved. Then, that person will need to use that defense even more desperately.

Buffered consequences.

If you truly want to help a person grow, you must be prepared to give that person the opportunity to create his (her) decisions. You know that the only impediment to a person's use of his (her) creativity is the immensity of the task, inundating and eventually depleting the fuel of fulfilment. You, therefore, must be prepared to remove parts of the buffer just as you were prepared to remove parts of the problem by introducing the buffer in the first place. This, for example, is the act of gradually exposing a child to the demands of the modern world. It also is the act of exposing an adult, so that such a person can be more useful to the organization or community as the stresses of change continue to become more pervasive and more demanding.

You will have to be self affirmed to do this because you may be seen, not as allowing something that will have happened if you did not prevent it in the first place, but as the source of an unnecessary problem or consequence. They do not see the real consequence that their limited visions do not allow them to see. They see only the problem you have instigated or allowed to happen. Then, the resistances of the other person will more be directed at you rather than at the source of the pressure.

The following examples will, I hope, serve to illustrate what can be a method of management that may be considered to be too different from those we may have learned to use, either because we accepted them in deference to our teachers, or because we developed them in defiance of the experiences we may have had to endure.

Example 1. The unproductive adult. An adult in your charge refuses to offer more than the bare minimum despite your attempts to help and encourage him (her). As a result, that person continues to do a poor job at managing his (her) tasks. Nothing happens, but your greater vision tells you that you are saved only by circumstance. Something disastrous should have happened already. What do you do? You cannot wait for the repercussions to appear before you do something. You have attempted to facilitate, educate, and even affirm the person. Now, you must be the source of controlled consequences. You must provide a consequence that is less than what may happen, but greater than what is seen as appropriate to the person. This is a buffered consequence.

Now, that person will be motivated to reassess his (her) performance at the task, not because of his (her) greater understanding of the demands of the task, but because of his (her) fears of the consequences you represent

Example 2. The defiant child. Your child plays in the street. You know that there is a grave danger to this, danger which the child does not have the vision to understand. Facilitating the child is limited to what you can do when you are with him (her). You can request road bumps. You can divert traffic. You can stay in the street with your child so that you will be able to forestall the danger before it happens. Do not laugh at these solutions. Some people do go through such trouble. Yet, if you do so to the level that it becomes safe, you will be giving that child greater evidence that you are worrying unnecessarily, that there really is no danger.

Trying to educate him (her) does not go far as he (she) can logically discount all your arguments. The child believes that, because there are no cars visible to him (her) at the time he (she) is playing, there is no danger. Even when cars come by, the child may reason, the drivers slow down and stop when they see the children. Your child does not have the experience to know about drunk drivers or people who are distracted by personal worries.

You even try to affirm the child for other successes. You may emphasize your approval of his (her) occasional decisions to play in the back yard, or in the park while showing disapproval for playing in the street.

Whatever you do, the child still plays in the street. The real consequence is that your child may be killed. You cannot let that happen. Therefore, you decide to be the source of buffered consequences. You impose a discomfort on the child for disobeying you. This may take the form of a spank firm enough to make the point, without being a harsh punishment. The idea is not to hurt the child unnecessarily. It is to provide proof that there is a consequence to his (her) mismanagement of the issue. Instead of a spanking, if the child is old enough to let this be applicable, it may take the form of a removal of privileges.

In the perceptions of the child, this buffered consequence will be considered to be a severe discomfort. Only you will know that it is a less severe discomfort that the one the child cannot see, being hit by a car, for example. That child will be motivated to manage the situation appropriately, not because he (she) understands the gravity of the problem, but because he (she) understands the consequences that will come from you.

Contrary to some people's fears, this will not alienate the child against the parent. In fact, it allows any affirmation you may share for some other act to be more believable. The child knows that you are being honest, if only because you have shown that you will show your displeasure when you do not accept something else.

Example 3. The difficult adolescent. Adolescence is, perhaps, the most difficult time in anyone's life. It is the time when the body is going through so many changes that adolescents become confused about who they really are and where they really are going. It also is a time when their parents and other adults still see them as children while their peers see them as adults who should have full authority over their own lives. They are pulled in every direction, rarely knowing which is right.

Defiance, therefore, seems to be a natural behaviour for any adolescent because the solutions for one area of their world will always conflict with the problems in another. If, however, you will remember that this is the period of breaking out, a period of discovery when the world of people, places, and things that he (she) will have to face becomes more a part of his (her) life than is the more familiar world of the parent, you will begin to see a reason for the defiance. Their world is beginning to take on more immediate importance than the world of their parent's dreams, hopes, and ambitions.

Ideally, the transition should be gradual. You will find, however, that in this era of rapid change, the demands from their peers or from the work they are required to accomplish are so great that they are easily inundated. Then they will develop defenses, just to deal with these extreme stresses.

There are, therefore, two considerations you must make when dealing with what you may see as a defiant adolescent. The first is that the behaviour may be an appropriate solution for the pressure from a world you cannot experience, but one which is more important to him (her) than the one you can see. The second is that it may just be a defense required to survive in that world.

If it is the former, you are well advised to respect it, but encourage the adolescent to expand his (her) concerns to include the world beyond those immediate demands. If it is the latter, it becomes necessary for you to help that person deal with the issues that threaten him (her) in a more creative manner. You differentiate between them simply by trying to see the problems through his (her) eyes.

Be genuinely interested in understanding his (her) world, and make the effort to show that interest. We discussed this in the section under management through education. It is only when you truly can understand the stresses imposed on him (her) by his (her) world that you will be in the position to offer a solution that draws from your more developed creativity.

It is only after you have accepted that there are unique problems he (she) has to face, after you have made an effort to understand them, and after you have offered a solution that has been refused that you can assume that there is an inappropriate behaviour.

If he (she) wants to follow through with the behaviour regardless of your efforts to educate him (her) on the unseen consequences or circumvent the need for a defense with honest affirmation, you may have to allow him (her) to experience the consequences, and manage them. Too many parents harm their adolescents by protecting them from consequences that should influence their behaviour. Sometimes, you may have to offer a buffered consequence in order to discourage the person from doing what he (she) intended and so activate the consequences that might be extremely harmful

In the management through delegation, you may be seen as inconsiderate, or even pedagogic. If you are self accountable, you will accept this without prejudice, and continue to manage your responsibility with maturity and dignity. Just as it is wrong to do something which attempts to show accountability while creating a greater problem underneath, so too it is wrong to let another person suffer the emptiness of stagnation just so you can appear to be generous on the surface.

The four stages of effective management, facilitation, education, affirmation, and delegation do not always have to be applied in that order. Sometimes, it is necessary to assume that your dependents are mature thinkers, that they can do the job when it is given to them. Then, you may delegate at first. By doing that, you will have given them the opportunity to display the level at which they can function comfortably. By their defenses, you will recognize which people will need facilitation, which will benefit from education, and which will require affirmation. Then, you can be flexible enough to manage each person appropriately for his (her) abilities, and so get the most from people as the individuals they are.

Epilogue.

To manage effectively, therefore, there are two main points you must bear in mind. The first is that everyone may have been created equal.

You know, however, that everyone grows at an unequal pace, depending on the affirmation he (she) may have received to fuel his (her) creativity, and on the challenges he (she) was given to stimulate it. A healthy balance of these two can allow anybody to develop the momentum to be a successful manager. The second, therefore, is that it is never too late to provide this balanced growth.

Sometimes, you have to give what, to the observer, may be an imbalance. At some stages, you may be seen to give too much affirmation for the amount of the task. At other stages you may be seen to give too much task for the amount of affirmation. However, you know that the only way one can correct an imbalance is through the provision of a compensatory imbalance. To the observer, every person should be equally capable to every other person. If someone is not, then he (she) is perceived to have stagnated as a result of his (her) own disinterest. You must believe that it is not so.

What may seem to be too much affirmation, can be a drop in the ocean for the needy person. What may seem as too much responsibilities may only be the accumulated discards of the irresponsible or unaccountable person.

As a manager, you must create the vision for those who are too busy surviving the present to have a vision of the problems and consequences that lie ahead. That vision must allow you to have a plan for where you must take these people.

As a parent, for example, your duty is to lead your dependents into being capable adults, not to keep them as happy children, to teach them to be strong, not fight their battles for them. Yet, you must be prepared to stand behind them, to buffer them, so to speak, so that they will have consequences, but not as severe as the world will throw at them.

As an administrator, you need people who, eventually, can function independently and grow to meet the demands of the task, not tools that are simple extensions of yourself. Doing this will not necessarily make you popular. It, however, makes you effective. You will be doing what you can see as necessary for the greater good of the people you have been given the responsibility to manage.

Your vision also must take both the task and the person into account. Just as they do not have the vision for the changes that must be addressed in the task, they also do not always have enough vision for the changes that must be addressed in their own needs. You must be the source of their productivity as well as being the source of their well being. Just as you must push, you also must assign the breaks that they may not have the self management to take.

Remember, to your own self, be true. To what you accept as the other person, be honest.

FINIS CORONAT OPUS.

Bibliography

Baars, Conrad W., Terrure, Anna A.,: Healing the Unaffirmed.Alba House. New York. 1972.

Bohr Neils: Atomic Physics and Human Knowledge

Bohr Niels: Atomic Theory and the Nature of Consciousness. Cambridge University Press.

Born, Max: Einstein's Statistical Theories. Albert Einstein: Philosopher - Scientist. Cambridge University Press.

Bourke, Vernon J.: The Pocket Aquinas. Washington Square Press. 1960.

Broad, C. D. ed. McTaggart, J. & McTaggart, Ellis: The Nature of Existence. Cambridge University Press

Bronowski, Jan: The Ascent of Man. Macdonald Futura Publishers. 1973.

Davis, Allen F. and Woodman, Harold D.: Conflict and Consensus in Modern American History. D. C. Heath and Company. 1984.

De Goias Albert: Individual Development within a Dualistic Paradigm. Modelling and Simulation, Volume 14. School of Engineering, University of Pittsburg. 1983.

De Goias Albert: Individuality, Dualism, and Perception of Performance in an Insecure Reality. Modelling and Simulation, Volume 13. School of Engineering, University of Pittsburg. 1982.

UNDERSTANDING CHANGE

Everett, N. B. Functional Neuroanatomy. Lea & Febiger. 1971.

Freeman W. F., Watts, J.: Psychosurgery in the Treatment of Mental Disorders and Intractable Pain. Thomas. 1950.

Haldane, Elizabeth S., Ross, G. R. T., The Philosophical Works of Descartes. Cambridge University Press. 1979.

Haley, Jay: Advanced Techniques of Hypnosis and Therapy - Selected Papers of Milton H. Erickson M.D. Grune & Stratton. New York. 1967.

Martin, Bernice: A Sociology of Contemporary Cultural Change. Basil Blackwell, 1983

Pike, Nelson, ed.: Dialogues concerning natural religion/ David Hume. The Bobbs Merrill Company Inc. 1970.

Schlipp, Paul Arthur, ed.: Albert Einstein: Philosopher-Scientist. Cambridge University Press. London. 1982.

Selye, Hans: Stress Without Distress. Lippincott. New York. 1974.

Walker, Evan Harris: The Nature of Consciousness. Mathematical Biosciences. 1970.

INDEX